With best w
Dinah Livin
from
Peter Gould
28 November 1992

A LULL BETWEEN MONSOONS

A LULL BETWEEN MONSOONS

An experience of Malaysia

PETER GAULD

Illustrated by the author

ß

THE BURRELL PRESS
IPSWICH

For
JIM DIXON and DENIS HEWETT:
good neighbours both

First published in 1991 by The Burrell Press
PO Box 168, Ipswich, Suffolk IP2 8AQ, England

Copyright © Peter Gauld 1991
All rights reserved

British Library Cataloguing in Publication Data

Gauld, Peter
  A lull between monsoons: an experience
  of Malaysia.
  I. Title
  959.5053

ISBN 0-9517442-0-8

Photoset by Rowland Phototypesetting Ltd
Bury St Edmunds, Suffolk
Printed by St Edmundsbury Press Ltd
Bury St Edmunds, Suffolk

Contents

PART ONE

Townscape with Goats	9
The School	22
View from a Hill	34

PART TWO

Country Music at the Federal	53
Love in Pahang	72
A Meal in Rat Alley	84

PART THREE

The Variegation of Existence	101
Tinggol	115
The River	123
One Fruit of House	139

PART FOUR

A Spin with Mr Tan	155
Bread Pudding and Swiss Cheese	167
Speaking in Tongues at Telok Lipat	182
East Coast to East Coast	198

PART ONE

PART ONE

Townscape with Goats

From a deserted wooden market stall by the harbour I watched a couple of cats sauntering across an untidy strip of beach, weaving their way elegantly between the heaps of rocks where yellow-flowering cacti sprouted. What the cacti were doing in a part of the tropics with at least a hundred and thirty inches of rain a year I never managed to find out. An enormous shiny black bee lumbered round the lilac flowers of a milkweed bush. Overhead, a sea-eagle circled.

Beyond the cacti and the milkweed a small sailing ferry, assisted by a paddle, was making its unsteady way across to the fishing kampong on the far shore of the estuary. Behind the wooden houses of the kampong rose a line of steep hills densely fleeced with forest. There was a trace of pallid sunshine to enliven the scene that afternoon, which was particularly welcome as ever since my arrival a couple of days before it had been raining non-stop.

I had come to this small town on the east coast of the Malay peninsula to start a two-year contract as an English teacher. It was to be several days before I found a house to rent, so for the moment I had nothing to do except ruminate (as I was doing) by the harbour mouth, or go back to the echoing concrete Hotel Kasanya nearby, which was either beginning to fall apart or else had never been completed. Or perhaps both.

The town, like the state of Trengganu as a whole, was predominantly Malay, but the harbour-side cross-roads which made up its urban centre consisted of a cluster of Chinese shops. Dogs with pendulous udders lay comatose in Jalan Besar, the High Street, ignoring the goats which strolled briskly past. Hens with clusters of chicks in tow foraged in the roadside rubbish skips. Apart from the Hotel

Kasanya the buildings of the town were of weathered wood, with overhanging metal roofs. The tallest structure in sight was a huge hoarding advertising 'Endless Love', starring Brooke Shields. Behind this you could glimpse an array of fishing boats at anchor in the harbour.

About the whole place hung the melancholy of a small dilapidated tropical town on a long afternoon in the monsoon season. The inhabitants – goats, cats, chickens, Chinese dogs, Malay fishermen – wandered round with a certain self-assurance. Sitting by the estuary staring across at the steep shaggy woods of the far shore I felt a little out of things.

From my second-floor room in the hotel, when I walked back there to get a marginally different perspective on things, I could see the breakers rolling in, charged with orange-brown sand, from the South China Sea. Brown breakers, white horses, grey sea: it looked like the sea I had grown up beside on another East Coast far to the north, in Suffolk.

In the event I stayed for only four nights at the Kasanya. It was not a long acquaintance, but even so I felt I had seen enough of its attractions: the walls of my room, which were bare and white except for various uncompleted bits of wiring which protruded here and there, the *kiblat* arrow on the ceiling which pointed towards Mecca for the benefit of Muslim guests performing their prayers, the prominent handprint on the bathroom wall and the list of regulations on the door. I was particularly struck by No. 12: FOR SANITATION SAKE, VISITORS ARE KINDLY ASKED TO REFRAIN FROM SPITTING ON THE FLOOR. I refrained.

In the evening I sauntered out in search of somewhere to eat. I wanted to find somewhere a shade more appealing than the little Indian bar-café next to the hotel. I had sat here earlier in the day drinking sludgy Malaysian coffee and watching a large rat lolloping slowly across the floor into the shadows. A light shower of rain came on as I was passing a Malay foodstall. I took it as an omen and sat down on the wooden bench.

There were spirit lamps hanging from the roof, flickering

and flaring in the warm monsoon wind, and the corrugated metal clattered as it was shaken. Malay children wandered round in the shadows and the two women grilling the satay gave me a friendly smile. When I had eaten I launched into my first real Malay conversation.

It was a limited kind of exchange, but your first conversation in any foreign language represents a kind of initiation. Never mind the trivia you are attempting to discuss, or the huge gaps in your elementary vocabulary which are revealed three times in every sentence. It is still a significant moment.

'I am a *cikgu*,' I said, since they were obviously curious, 'a teacher, from the Science School – *Sekolah Sains* – and I am *dari Inggeris*, from England.'

'Oh,' said one of the mothers, pointing to the twelve-year-old, 'she goes to the other school.'

'Yes,' said the little girl proudly, 'and my teacher is Mr Martin.'

'Aha,' I said, '*saya baru beli basikal daripada Martin*. I've just bought a bicycle from Martin.'

The other woman asked: '*Sudah berapa lama di sini?* How long have you been here?'

A mental block intervened. I got as far as '*Tiga* . . .' (i.e. three), but failed to make the connection for 'day'.

'*Tiga tahun?*' they asked. '*Tiga bulan?* Three years? Three months?'

At last the right plug slipped into its socket. 'No,' I said, '*tiga hari*.'

'Three days, eh? Well well . . .' I felt as though I were being congratulated on some marvellous accomplishment. There was something both welcome and welcoming about their smiles and the warm flaring light of the lamps. Wind-blown flames danced on the kebab sticks as they grilled. I could hear the muezzin calling from the mosque in the distance. For a tentative moment, struggling to light my pipe in the wind and sipping Nescafé under the flapping awning, I felt at home.

But the pipe refused to light, and I was forced to take it

back to the unwelcoming shelter of Room 312 with its *kiblat* arrow and the handprint on the bathroom wall.

The house I moved to was not much more than half a mile away, down a bumpy side-road behind the Telekom headquarters. It was raised on concrete supports about four feet above the ground in the local manner, except for the kitchen-bathroom end at the back which was down at ground level. A railed concrete flight of steps led up to the front door.

The house was something like a wooden barn with a corrugated metal roof, set within what I would have called a small garden, but in that part of the world is referred to as a compound. This consisted of a lawn of coarse tropical grass surrounded by overgrown shrubs, notably allamandas with flaring butter-yellow trumpets and a clump of bushes on which some previous tenant had wired little hanging orchids. These burst into purple flower once a year.

Around all these was a collapsing fence made of the same corrugated metal panels as the roof. Every couple of months a section of this would collapse altogether and I would have to rush out into the compound to drive away the inescapable goats which would find their way in, guided by some kind of bush telegraph. Bearing in mind the popular reputation of this uncritical animal they were surprisingly fastidious, ignoring the coarsely overgrown shrubs which half-blocked the gate and making their way without hesitation towards whatever rarities I was attempting to grow in sheltered pots by the front door steps.

Until recently the house had been the Elim Pentecostal Church, run by a pair of missionaries from Finland, Sisters Paukku and Hokkanen. It was partitioned down the middle with thin plywood. One half had been the church proper, the other the minister's living-quarters. I took the deconsecrated half, and my colleague Jim moved into the other: the vicarage, so to speak. Jim was a plump, genially grumbling Yorkshireman a few years younger than myself, who had just spent a couple of years teaching in Japan. We got on well, which was a good thing because the thin partition wall did not make for privacy. I soon found out that Jim liked to listen to the BBC World Service late at night, and snored. I never asked what he might have found out about me.

There was nothing much about the interior of the house, with its wooden room-partitions which stopped well short of the ceiling, which suggested any kind of church I had ever come across, except perhaps the height of its ceiling and the prevailing gloom which resulted from dark woodwork and inadequate windows. The only remnant of its former consecrated existence was a chart which was still pinned in place on Jim's living-room wall when we moved in. At the top it said in large letters A CHART OF THE COURSE OF TIME FROM ETERNITY TO ETERNITY. Creation was represented as spreading from interlocking spheres marked CHAOS and EDEN. The present age appeared as the Fourth Dispensation, otherwise the Day of Grace.

In the next age (the Day of Trouble) came the Great Tribulation, Satan Cast Down and the Seven-Sealed Book Opened. Further on still was the Day of God and THE GREAT WHITE THRONE. There was also a Lake of Fire marked for 'whosoever' (as the chart ominously phrased it) 'was not found written in the Book of Life.' It was all a bit like something out of Blake, one of those Prophetic Books which only the true enthusiast ever gets round to reading. You expected to see Urizen or Enitharmon popping up in it somewhere. In one corner, in small letters, credit for this effusion was claimed by the Bible Truth Depot of Neptune, New Jersey, whose name conjured up images of some vast underwater warehouse.

Jim remained untroubled by this gloomy piece of eschatology. I would hear him whistling tunelessly to himself through the thin partition wall. The melodic line of his whistling would follow the general contours of some familiar tune, but the intervals were most peculiar.

Sometimes I would hear a more melodious kind of whistling. Opposite our zinc-fenced compound were a few other wooden houses with Chinese families living in them. These houses were almost hidden among lush mango trees, and sometimes looking out of the small front windows on a somnolent weekend afternoon I would hear a plaintive contralto whistle and glimpse an oriole, a flash of pure, startlingly intense yellow, darting from one dense mass of foliage to another.

My journal entries relating to that first period in the house have as much in them about natural history as they do about human life. I had never come across anything like it before. A couple of years later, reading the naturalist Alfred Russel Wallace's nineteenth-century classic *The Malay Archipelago*, I was struck by his reference to 'a glorious spot . . . which will always live in my memory as exhibiting the insect life of the tropics in unexampled luxuriance.' He was referring to a small island in the Moluccas, but I was instantly reminded of that rather gloomy house off Jalan Nibong behind the Telekom headquarters, with its two outdoor privies and sapling mango tree.

The insect life there was alternately menacing and breathtaking. There were butterflies of every size and colour, carpenter bees, mosquitoes, cockroaches, seething masses of ants. More disturbing creatures surfaced now and then. There were three of us British teachers at the Science School to begin with. The third was a big morose self-contained man I shall call Desmond. Desmond had a slow hulking walk and the most evasive eyes I had ever come across. They flickered from side to side as he spoke to you, like those of a settler in the Old West, hemmed in by advancing Redskins, despairingly scanning the horizon on the off-chance that the U.S. Cavalry might be out on manoeuvres.

The two of us had previously been assigned by the company to share a room in the Kuala Lumpur hotel they were using for our three-week orientation course, and Desmond, who was an insomniac, had not endeared himself to me by smoking large rank cigars in bed during the night. I am partial to a large rank cigar myself at the right moment, but not in an air-conditioned room at one o'clock in the morning.

He had also rigged up his Sony Walkman to two tiny speakers, a trick I had not seen before, and spells of relaxation in the hotel were enlivened (from Desmond's point of view) by the tinny blaring of the current UK Top Forty pop hits. Desmond would sink back on to his bed with a sigh of relief as the thin metallic screeching rose above the muted sound of traffic in Jalan Bukit Bintang six floors below and the atmosphere thickened with acrid smoke.

'There's something reassuring about pop music,' he said once. 'Don't you think?'

He was one of those people who keep the world at a safe distance – intentionally or otherwise – by surrounding themselves with their own fug.

Desmond had moved from the Kasanya into a separate kampong house a mile or so away. He was not a sociable person, so I was surprised when he called late one evening. His entrance was dramatic.

In the Sherlock Holmes story called 'The Lion's Mane' there is a schoolmaster who staggers across the threshold in agony groaning *'Brandy . . .'* and then collapses. Desmond did not collapse across the threshold, but it was clear that he was suffering. Like the man in Conan Doyle's story he had been stung by something poisonous. In 'The Lion's Mane' the culprit was a rare and dangerous kind of jellyfish; in Desmond's case it was a giant centipede. He had been in the outside privy behind his house in the darkness, and the centipede had been coiled round the length of hosepipe attached to the tap.

It had bitten him on the ankle. In the circumstances I suppose he might have been even less fortunate.

He was on his way back home now from the clinic near my house, armed with anti-histamine pills and a variety of ointments. Despite all these he was obviously in considerable pain. It was the first time I had seen this anti-social and faintly sinister individual as vulnerable, and therefore human. In the absence of brandy I gave him tea. There was not much else I could do.

Giant centipedes were the one local life-form I never

managed to conquer my loathing of. They grew to at least seven or eight inches, perhaps more; it is hard to be exact since like snakes or the fish which get away from the angler they can easily be taken for longer than they actually are. I had already killed one at a friend's house in Kuantan down the coast by battering it with a size ten rubber flip-flop. This is a technique not recommended by experts as the creatures (which are almost indestructible, as well as sinuously jointed and incredibly fast in their movements) are quite capable of doubling back over the sides of the sandal and stinging your hand.

Months later I found one in my own kitchen sink, which doubled as a wash-basin. It scuttled out of a fold in my face-flannel, legs threshing, like the backbone of a substantial kipper come to life, as I was about to clean my teeth by the inadequate light of a single overhead bulb. The electric kettle had recently come to the boil, and in a spasm of fear and loathing I poured the contents over the centipede. A neighbour's chickens enjoyed the remains the next morning. It seemed to me after a couple of months in Malaysia that even St Francis of Assisi might have modified his attitudes in the tropics.

The traditional local prophylactic was sulphur. Jim had obtained a large supply of this from the school science laboratory and scattered it liberally around the perimeter of the house, a yellow trail like some sort of festive offering to the household gods. The centipede had side-stepped this *cordon sanitaire* by crawling up the waste-pipe.

As far as insect-life was concerned I found it easier to feel benevolent towards the large hawk-moths which sometimes came into the house. A Malay colleague at school told me that in Malay folklore a moth in the house means visitors to come. In the event there were a number of these, beginning with a straggle of cats which soon came to see Jim and myself as a soft touch where saucers of evaporated milk and platefuls of leftovers were concerned. There were also various human unfortunates who presumably used to come for handouts and reassurance (in the same way as the cats) in the days when No. 4F Jalan Nibong was the Elim church.

The first was a gentle, harmless (as far as I could tell) middle-aged Chinese by the name of Chia Joon Thian who appeared barefoot and silently, in the manner of an apparition, as I was making coffee in the kitchen around sunset one evening. He wore nothing but a pair of baggy trousers and a none-too-clean white vest. I could see a bicycle propped against the gate outside.

'Di chut?' enquired Mr Chia, smiling. Or at least that was what it sounded like. I was not used to local pronunciation yet.

'I'm sorry?'

'The chu'ch. Where is now?'

I told him it had moved, but I did not know where to. Mr Chia appeared in no hurry to continue his search, so I offered him coffee. We sat drinking it in silence in the living-room while Mr Chia smiled with vague dislocated benevolence around him. His conversation was limited.

Feeling slightly at a loss, I picked up my pipe from the side-table and poked around inside it with a penknife. In a moment Mr Chia was beside me. Visions of sudden knife-murders flashed through my mind. The *parang*, the jungle knife, is a favourite weapon in that part of the world, and although my own experience of Malaysia was of a relatively crime-free country you might think differently if you were to read the New Straits Times every day. I wondered fleetingly if I had offended against some Chinese *tabu*.

But Mr Chia merely smiled his dislocated smile, reached down gently and put the pipe in my mouth. The brief tropical twilight was deepening, and picking up my lighter he lit the candle-stub which had been left on the table in case of power-cuts (which happened frequently). We sat smiling vaguely at each other by its wavering light, drinking coffee and eating biscuits. In the end, still smiling and without having uttered a single further word, he ambled off to his bicycle.

A few days later it was the turn of another Christian Chinese, a younger and brisker man called Peter Tan who appeared in the doorway as I was relaxing after school.

'Hallo. Are you the new pastor?'

I explained, not for the first or last time, that the church had moved, and finished up lending him ten dollars. I never saw him again.

Aside from Jim, my neighbours were also Chinese. I remember an Australian commenting on the shock he had had on first coming across the Chinese in South-East Asia. He had been a teacher in Australia, and in the schools of New South Wales at least the ethnic Chinese were a byword for quietness, decorum, obsessive hard work. Their children were the kind of pupils teachers dream of: softly-spoken, obedient, polite, producing every piece of written work on time with legible handwriting and amazingly few mistakes.

'But over here,' he said – 'jeez, I suppose they haven't got to bother about showing they're better than the Europeans, so they let themselves go . . . I mean, have you heard the *noise* they make, for God's sake?'

It was the reaction a South American might have, for example, coming to Britain for the first time and seeing not the self-contained, possibly snobbish or exclusive but at least respectably middle-class English minority of Santiago or Buenos Aires but the football hooligans and skinheads of Ruritania-on-Thames itself.

For several weeks I heard and saw very little of the family across the lane, the one whose pewter-grey wooden house was all-but-hidden by the mango trees where golden orioles swooped and fluted. There were glimpses of purple bougainvillea through the greenery, and an ornate wooden gable above the front window. It looked an idyllic place, what you could see of it, much more so than No. 4F with its collapsing tin fence and uncompromising roof-line. You imagined it, English suburban style, being called 'The Mangoes', Oriole Lane. It was the sort of house which should have belonged to a young couple deeply in love, or a serene elderly lady with a passion for birds and gardening.

One evening, at that magical hour when the tropical light briefly softens before everything is swallowed up in deepening twilight, Jim knocked on the kitchen wall and interrupted my preparations for an omelette. 'Come and listen to this,' he said. 'I've never heard anything like it.'

I went round (our two back doors were adjacent) and followed him through to his front room. From here there was a slightly better view of the house across the lane. I could see nothing out of the ordinary.

'What is it?'

'Listen. They'll start again any moment.'

I listened. There came a high-pitched screech, followed by a crash. There followed another screech – a woman's voice, but a different one this time – then another answering crash.

'What on earth are they doing?'

Jim's face had a look of malicious glee. 'Throwing crockery. They must have got through half a Welsh dresserful by now. I'm surprised you couldn't hear it at the back.'

The screeching grew more rapid as the plates flew thick and fast. Crash – Eeeyaaah! Smash – Aaaiyeee! Perhaps (we speculated) it was a monumental disagreement between mother and daughter-in-law. If so, the husband was either hiding under a bed or (sensibly in the circumstances) out for a drink. We stayed there listening as twilight deepened into darkness. It was impossible to ignore the noise. The two women (whoever they really were) must have gone on hurling crockery until there was nothing left in the kitchen to hurl. After that evening neither of us ever heard an untoward sound from the house again.

The neighbours on my side of the house were a slum family of the most unregenerate kind, the kind you imagine London social workers despairing of. There were a number of children; I never managed to work out how many. None of them responded to any kind of greeting. On still nights the surf of the South China Sea was clearly audible on Telok Lipat beach less than a quarter of a mile away, but at times the screaming of the small boy next door would rise shrilly to drown it as his mother – to judge by the sound of disturbed furniture – kicked him around the house.

I saw him attack her once in return. It was an impressive display of flailing hysterical fury, but he never stood a chance against her. She was a huge glowering woman who spread and sagged. I never heard her utter a word except in a penetrating screech.

The overgrown shrubs behind the tin fence obscured the fact that their house, which like mine stood on supports four feet above the ground, rose from a thick layer of discarded plastic containers, soft drink packets and rusting tin cans. Jim once rescued a small battered-looking kitten only a few weeks old from the children there, who were freely expressing their innocent little selves by throwing it around the filthy garden like a frisbee. When Jim rescued it, the kitten was only half-alive – its hindquarters were paralysed – but it managed to raise its head for long enough to lick up some milk. When I stroked it, it produced a tiny rasping purr. It was dead in the morning. After this my sympathy for the youngest boy was more limited.

A couple of months later I went away to Kuala Lumpur, three hundred miles away, to attend a company course for several weeks. When I came back I found that Mr Rasul the landlord had been on a Clean-up-the-Kampong campaign. The wooden room-partitions in my house, which had only recently been put in after the migration of the church, and which were cheap and shoddy compared with the rest of the woodwork, had been painted with aluminium paint. As a result the front room now looked like the living-quarters of a Third World spaceship.

I did my best not to show my horror. 'But why metallic paint?'

'Keep away termite.'

'But couldn't you have used varnish or something? It's wood, after all. It could look really nice.'

Rasul looked at me blankly. In the developing world, how could any house not made of concrete be said to 'look really nice'?

'Metal paint better.'

He had also, not before time, kicked out the slum family next door. Before leaving, they had taken their ill-directed revenge by cutting my telephone cable.

The family who soon moved in to replace them, a young couple with an endearing toddler, were a great improvement, except that they shared what seems to be the universal Chinese horror of silence. To their noisy stereo they subsequently added the refined torture of an electronic gadget which played 'Nick-nack, Paddywack, give the dog a bone' over and over again in a shrill synthesised whistle. It was one of the most penetrating sounds I had ever heard, so it seemed hard to believe what all the evidence suggested, namely that it was intended to send the baby to sleep.

Whenever they switched it on at the same time as the stereo, on which they liked to listen to pulsing disco music, Nick-nack Paddywack would win hands down. It was almost as bad as sharing a hotel room with Desmond.

SOUTH CHINA SEA LULLABY

Water-apples plop from the branch
Within the night's stillness. Under
The tin roof the resident doves clatter.
Lightning flickers, but no thunder –
   And no sleep, for that matter

Jackfruit, papayas, coconuts
Hang gravid on each laden tree.
The voice of the child next door relentlessly crying
Resists the hushing of the sea
   (Nothing, at least, is dying).

Beside the privy the lovesick cats
Are copulating where they roam.
Absent alike are nymph and satyr
From the South China Sea's Islamic foam:
   The mocking geckos chatter.

Out there in the foam at the world's edge
It slips away once again, the land,
From the wave's dying grasp where the colours of
    sunset
Long ago drained away in the sand:
  Sleep, says the sea. Forget.

The School

The Secondary Science School where I had come to teach was about three miles out of town along the coast, via a busy main road (busy, that is, by rural East Coast standards) along which huge timber lorries roared well into the night. They did not gladden my heart when I cycled out in that direction, either to reach the school or to explore the Forest Reserve several miles further along, but they probably gladdened the heart of my landlord Mr Rasul.

Rasul in Malay, via Arabic, means 'Sent by God', but this has not prevented my landlord from doing a stretch in prison. I never found out the details of this, but it did not appear to have lowered his standing in the community. The normal modern Malaysian Malay equivalent of 'Mr' is *Encik* (or as it used to be spelt, *enche*'), but my new Chinese neighbours left notes on their door for *Tuan* Rasul, which is a much more respectful mode of address. He was a bland, fleshy, rather Levantine-looking man who spoke English in a fluent gabble which I often found hard to understand, as though (in painter's terms) he were using an impressionist technique of fluid brush-strokes to portray the basic phonetics of the English language.

He owned all the houses in the immediate area, and was extremely rich. Aside from rents his money came from timber, so that at least some of the lorries laden with enormous tree-trunks which narrowly avoided sweeping my bicycle into the roadside scrub on their way from the logging concessions of Ulu Kelantan must have represented profits for Mr Rasul.

The school had only been built eighteen months before. Its grounds stretched from the main road as far as the quieter coast road which ran in parallel for a few miles immediately behind the beach. A gate gave access to this, but I never saw it open. It was a boarding school – a residential school, as people there preferred to say – and the pupils were not free to wander.

The entire site had formerly been a coconut plantation, and although a mop-headed line of palms still screened the coast road there was not a single one to be seen on the acres of flat prairie which made up the school compound. 'Couldn't they have left a few?' I asked one of the local teachers.

I received a look of blank incomprehension. '*Coconut* palms?' It was as though a visiting Greenlander in England, impressed by the intricate massive goblets of Savoy cabbage growing in a market garden, had asked why such things were not planted more often in park flower-beds. To the average educated Malaysian the coconut palm is a functional unaesthetic thing, a sort of high-rise cabbage. Its products are appreciated, but as a feature of the landscape it is considered embarrassingly rustic, an indication of inadequate 'development'.

Jim, Desmond and I were there to prepare sixth-form students for the American TOEFL exam (Teaching of English as a Foreign Language), which both American and Australian universities accept as a gauge of proficiency for entrance purposes. Or at least that was the original idea; the Ministry of Education changed its mind a number of times about what it wanted. It was all very complicated. Language is inseparable from politics in Malaysia, and also from economics. Competent English gets students into respected overseas universities, but it is also seen as a threat to the updated and officially reshaped Malay or *Bahasa Malaysia* which is the national language. In colonial times, in other words until well into the sixties, English was widespread in what was then Malaya, at least among urban people. Then came independence, and the government saw its opportunity to assert the Malay claim to national dominance by emphasising *Bahasa Malaysia* at the expense of English. The idea was that this would help the rural Malays to catch up with their urban cousins and particularly with the more enterprising Chinese and Indians.

So standards of English slipped among the Malays. Why should they bother, after all? Their own language, give or take a few new official coinages, was now the national one. The colonial era was over. Changes in the education system would soon force the Chinese and Indians and Sarawakians to learn proper Malay, whether they wanted to or not. At the same time the Government began to notice that their cherished Malay students were beginning to find difficulty in reaching the standard of English necessary to get into foreign universities in Britain, the United States, Canada, Australia, New Zealand. The pendulum had swung too far. It was time to bring in some foreign expertise to redress the balance. Hence our arrival.

We were working not directly for the Government but for a British company which had been awarded the contract to provide teachers and run the project. Indirectly, of course, we were Government employees. Working in effect for two sets of masters had its awkward moments, but I never had any personal quarrel with the British company. On the whole, I felt, they did a humane job in difficult circumstances.

The problems of language policy did not end there. In the intensely religious states of Trengganu and Kelantan there were a number of people who felt strongly that English should not be taught at all, that Arabic should be made the second language of the country. Malays should be fluent in the language God had chosen for his final revelation to mankind, not the language of sex, drugs, rock 'n' roll and infidel Christianity. We were always being made to feel on the East Coast that we were walking a tightrope, passing on functional language skills (vocabulary, grammar, taking

notes from lectures) without any cultural content whatever. It is an impossible task, when you think about it. You cannot treat a living human language as a pure code of communication, like Esperanto or Fortran.

Some people saw everything we did, just as much as everything we conspicuously avoided doing, as a threat to their own culture. One of my Australian colleagues who came half-way through the first year was once seen sitting on the edge of a table in the resource room among a group of sixth-formers. We discovered belatedly that the news of this had passed like wildfire around the local teachers. They were shocked. It was almost as though a teacher had been found making sexual advances to one of his pupils.

'But what on earth is wrong with sitting on the edge of the table?'

'But you cannot! It is dangerous. It teaches the students to *show disrespect.*'

The political and economic ramifications grew more complex during the two years I was there. American universities were seen as an attractive destination by the Government. Their capacity, after all, was enormous. On the other hand, putting all your student eggs in one academic basket came to be seen (reasonably enough) as having its dangers. The Government decided to diversify. Britain had never quite lost its academic prestige, but Dr Mahathir (who had never made any secret of his dislike for the British) was angry with Mrs Thatcher because in 1980 she had decided to make overseas students pay full fees. It was a decision which had far-reaching consequences, many of them unforeseen. In retaliation, Mahathir had implemented a Government 'Buy British Last' policy. It extended to university courses as well as to heavy machinery and office supplies.

Australia, the senior officials at the Ministry must have thought as they scanned the atlas, looked an attractive alternative. It was close enough to Malaysia, and the students would not be so likely to freeze to death in winter as in Manchester or Illinois. It was a pity about those worrying reports of anti-Asian racism in Sydney and Melbourne. What about New Zealand, then? Nice little country, splendid scenery, no threat to anyone, but too small to absorb more than a few Malaysian students. But what's this? Datuk, have you seen the exchange rates? The pound has fallen so low that even bearing in mind Mrs Thatcher's extortionate demands we could still afford to send a fair number to Britain . . .

The students were amazingly patient in the face of all this. Before they started they were told they were being sent on a course to get them into high school, and subsequently university, in Australia. Later it was hinted that they might stay in Malaysia instead. At the end of the year their exam results were concealed from them. They (like their teachers) ended up being treated as so much impersonal raw material in some vast manufacturing process whose aim was to produce, say, X civil engineers in 1988. And the material was not expected to object if those controlling it decided to experiment with the manufacturing process half-way through.

Nor were the European teachers expected to object – or even comment on anything out-of-the-way – when we were informed two days before leaving Kuala Lumpur for our schools that the Ministry had decided at the last moment to economise by not buying any books for the course. Or when we were kept waiting until November to hear whether or not we would still be needed in January of the following year.

'Listen,' said a colleague to me during that opening orientation course in Kuala Lumpur, 'don't start worrying about all this high-falutin' academic garbage they keep feeding us. Aims and objectives and bloody communication skills my left armpit. I wouldn't mind betting that as soon as we get out to whatever mosquito-infested shanty-town they're posting us to, we'll realise there's no point taking a single bloody thing seriously.'

He lasted less than a year in Malaysia. Slowly it began to filter through to the school that he was a bottle-of-whisky-before-breakfast man, and when he strolled down the main street of his small town one morning to buy some razor-blades without having remembered to put any clothes on, the company was obliged to decant him on to a plane back to London.

He was the one Jim had shared a hotel room with during the same course, while I was billeted with Desmond. Jim and I swapped horror stories about it one day.

'I think you win,' I said. 'On points.'

'Everybody thought I was exaggerating at the time. But he was a nice bloke, all the same, if you didn't have to share a room with him. Apparently the kids at school all loved him.'

In the meantime I was more preoccupied with settling into 4F-1 Jalan Nibong than with the shifting priorities of the Malaysian educational system. Rasul (at a price) had provided me with a bed, but that was all. Over the next few weeks I tried (never entirely convincingly) to turn the place into a comfortable home with the addition of an elegant rattan suite from the local workshop, some lengths of colourful batik material draped over the room-partitions and a wooden side-lamp to soften the effect of the glaring strip-lights which seem to be almost universal in Malaysian houses.

All this took longer than it might have done for three reasons: because the local bank took ten days to process and cash the 'out-station' cheques the three of us had been given in Kuala Lumpur; because Chinese New Year intervened two days after our arrival at the school and every commercial establishment in the town (even the Hotel Kasanya) shut for at least a week for an orgy of family reunions and the exchange of *ang pows*; and not least, because of the endless rain. On the 24th of February Jim saw a notice at the elegant Tanjong Jara Hotel a few miles up the coast: MONSOON SEASON OVER, WATER SPORTS AVAILABLE. Unfortunately the weather gods took umbrage at this presumption on the part of the Tourist Development Corporation, and after a couple of sunny days the deluges resumed. The resident bullfrogs, which had briefly gone into hiding, returned joyfully to the flooded school playing-fields to disturb my typing of stencils with their creaky monotonous croaking.

I asked a Malay colleague how much longer the rain was likely to go on for. The north-east monsoon season on that coast runs from November to April, but according to what I had been told that was not supposed to mean non-stop rain for the whole six months. It was more likely to mean deluging rain in November and December, then a much drier spell, then further deluges in April or thereabouts in anticipation of the change of season.

'It's the beginning of March,' I said in the aggrieved voice of an Englishman who assumes that only his own rain-shrouded island is cursed with an unpredictable climate, that everywhere else in the world seasons and rainfall patterns follow the dictates of the tourist brochures and the blue bar-charts in the geography textbooks. 'We came here in late January, and it's hardly stopped since then.'

Ismail shrugged. He looked completely unconcerned. 'This year maybe double monsoon.'

Malays seem quite to like rain. It means cool weather, and

nobody in the Asian tropics, except lunatic Westerners, ever objects to that.

Desmond came round once to 4F to see how Jim and I were settling in. As he tugged at his bristling moustache his gaze fell on the wooden table-lamp I had bought in Kuala Trengganu, the State capital, the previous week.

'How much 'dyou pay for that? My God, you were rooked. It's only turned wood. All you need is a lathe. I wouldn't have given half that much for it.'

He was no more appreciative of the rattan cane settee, armchairs and glass-topped tables. 'Can't think how they dare charge so much for that. It's only bloody bamboo, after all.'

'Actually, Desmond, it isn't, it's a kind of climbing palm, and as it only grows in the forest it's getting harder and harder –'

Desmond waved a meaty hand in dismissal. 'No, no, just bamboo. Ought to be cheap enough. Bloody rip-off if you ask me.'

Desmond was good at putting what might be called the reductionist viewpoint. Malaysia uses some of its abundant tin to make ornamental pewterware, some of it remarkably elegant. I once suggested buying some when he was wondering what to take back to England as a present.

'Selangor pewter? It's only bloody tin. I don't know how they have the cheek to charge so much for it. You might just as well buy a baked-bean can.'

He was soon to be the cause of a great deal of embarrassment to everyone except himself. Jim and I sometimes used to drink coffee together at the open-air tables of the school canteen. Sitting there enjoying the glucose 'lift' of a cup of coffee made with condensed milk and watching the antics of the brisk, cocky, mischievous-looking grey-and-yellow mynahs which the Malays call *gembala kerbau* or 'buffalo herdsmen' made a change from typing stencils.

I arrived one morning to see Jim absorbed in what looked like a very serious discussion with Rosniyah, one of the Malay teachers. Rosniyah had stood out ever since we had come to the school, partly because her manner was unusually welcoming and friendly, partly because she was the only one of the Malay women teachers who wore no head-covering at all. There were one or two others almost as daring who paid lip-service to local Muslim etiquette by wearing only a colourful headscarf, but the rest wore the complete *tudong*, like a nun's wimple, with something like a tight-fitting woollen balaclava underneath to make sure no wisp of seductive black hair strayed to tempt weak-minded men.

Rosniyah had spent several years in Manchester studying chemical engineering, spoke fluent English and tended to be delegated with the job of passing on messages from the Malay staff to the trio of Europeans.

I fetched my glass of coffee and joined them. 'Why so serious?'

Rosniyah was evasive. 'It's . . . well, I think *you* ought to tell him, Jim. I don't think I can say it twice.'

'Good God,' I said, 'is it something to do with me?'

'No, no, not at all . . . go on, Jim.'

Jim turned to me. On his normally jovial face, with its snub nose and sizeable moustache, was a look I could not decipher. I realised as he spoke that he was torn between shocked embarrassment and the desire to roar with laughter.

'Well, I'm a Yorkshireman, so I suppose I ought to be able to call a spade a bloody shovel. It's Desmond. He's got B.O.'

'I know he has. I didn't realise anyone else had noticed it.'

'Well, the local teachers have. They've sent poor Rosniyah here to get us to do something about it.'

There seemed to be no very immediate comment I could make. Rosniyah, who had been visibly shuffling with embarrassment, went back upstairs to the staffroom. Jim and I looked at each other and collapsed with laughter. A mynah, swaggering across the table in search of some discarded grains of rice, cocked its head to one side and stared at us in puzzlement.

'The bloody idiot,' said Jim. 'Now he's landed us with the problem when it's his B.O.'

'It's one of those indirect societies, isn't it? No confrontations. Not the sort of thing you'd expect an Asian to tell someone else face to face.'

'It's not just Asians. It's going to be bloody embarrassing for *us*. It's bad enough if it's your best friend. I hardly know the bloke. The trouble is, they're such fastidious people, and he really is pretty ripe. I mean, my God, for them to have got as far as sending Rosniyah to tell us . . .'

'I suppose it's one of those community things, isn't it? Everybody belongs to one here. Malays do things for other Malays. Chinese do things for other Chinese. They expect us to sort out our community problem together. We must all look alike to them, anyway.'

'I don't look like Desmond,' said Jim. 'Not even to a Malay. And I certainly don't smell like him.'

'So which of us is going to draw the short straw, then?'

'The Company made you the co-ordinator for the group,' said Jim with an air of decision. 'I think you ought to do it. *Noblesse oblige* and all that.'

I meditated, sipping sweet glutinous coffee. 'I suppose I could try. Got any tactful suggestions?'

'How about putting a bar of Lifebuoy on his desk?'

It was a problem neither of us ever managed to solve. Some weeks later we put it to the Regional Project Director who called regularly from the company office in Kuala Lumpur to see how things were going. He was a tall, elegant, gentlemanly Englishman who exuded an air of cool competence.

'Yes, I can see it's a bit of an awkward situation for you. I'll have a word with him, don't you worry.'

Jim and I breathed a sigh of relief, but the rejoicing was premature. The Regional Project Director was a man of genuine accomplishments. He was a dab hand at interviewing candidates for the job in London. He was capable of spending hours closeted in discussion with Malaysian educational officials without batting an eyelid. He could even remain visibly cool and composed in his grey safari suit with the temperature at 33 in the shade and the humidity near saturation point. Coping with this particular problem, though, was beyond him.

I never managed to find a way of conveying the message to Desmond, though I did get as far as doing some research. Apparently in East Africa, where he had spent several years, there is a malevolent species of fly which lays its eggs in wet washing. When you eventually put on your now-dry shirt the eggs hatch and produce tiny grubs which burrow into your skin. Desmond told me about this, in distasteful but fascinating detail.

'Burrow under your skin. They eat you alive. It's true.'

Later, back in England, I checked with a girl who had grown up in what is now Zambia. 'That's right,' she said. 'But it wasn't really that much of a problem. You just had to iron every single thing when you took it in from the line. That way you made sure you killed all the eggs.'

In fact this insect does not exist in South-East Asia (it must be one of the very few which does not), but Desmond remained unconvinced of this. Careful habits once learned are hard to lose. Unfortunately he never seemed to have acquired the habit of using an iron. Terrified of exposing his wet washing to the marauding insect-life of the open air, he dried it in a cramped airless kitchen, and that may have been at the root of the trouble.

Certainly it was his clothes which seemed to be the cause. I could identify the smell which horrified the local teachers as that of sweaty clothes left to fester in a washing basket for several days in a hot humid climate. It was acrid and extraordinarily penetrating; how the source of it himself managed to be unaware of it I could never understand. Perhaps the cigars he smoked had dulled his sense of smell.

The teaching side of school life also had its bizarre moments. The Ministry, in its wisdom, had sent the students to their schools at the beginning of term even though their teachers would be spending the first three weeks on an orientation course in the capital. As a result they had simply ended up being left in their classrooms for days on end with nothing to do. It was no wonder their motivation had largely evaporated by the time we arrived.

The school authorities had found out that the most reliable way of keeping these seventeen-year-olds out of mischief was to show them videos. This practice tended to continue even after our arrival, so that you would sometimes turn up for a lesson to find an empty classroom. A brief search would run the class to earth in the projection room.

'What's happened to my lesson?'

'Sir, sir, *Cikgu* so-and-so show us video, sir.'

This happened the day after their return from the half-term break. A fat, bouncy, well-read girl called Wan Shariah had brought back a cassette of semi-literate brutality about a series of axe-murders called *Friday the Thirteenth Part Two*. I queried the wisdom of this choice with one or two of the local staff and met total incomprehension.

'Iss a good fillem. The student enjoy. I also.'

Around the same time, in a kind of ironic counterpoint, an informal school concert had to be cancelled because it was considered 'against religion' for girls to appear on the same platform as boys. When the English Language Society got under way later in the year we found that it was impossible to arrange any kind of singing, for the same reason. Apparently Muslim girls are permitted to listen to boys singing, but not vice versa. We began to realise that in East Coast Islam we were up against something (to put it tactfully) rather disconcerting.

At the very least it meant that the prevailing tone of things was oddly priggish. A sense of irony, still more a sardonic sense of humour, seems to be a purely Western defensive weapon. In East Asian societies, values are very much received and not questioned. It was all rather Victorian. True, the girls did not wear crinolines and tightly-laced corsets, but the ankle-length skirts, long tunics and shroud-like wimples which concealed everything except a pair of hands and a little round face peeping shyly out must have been just as constricting and (in that climate) even more unhygienic.

Around the same time, Jim and I were asked to adjudicate the English speechmaking contest. A tone of earnest seriousness prevailed, in both choice of topic and individual treatment. Only the non-stop chattering of the fellow fourth- and fifth-formers who made up the audience tended to work against this.

We listened, faces impassive, to Zaumadi on *The historian is as important as the scientist* ('First let me give you the definition of a historian'), Aniza on *A well-disciplined student reflects credit on his school and his country* ('Lastly I must say that to be disciplined is to be mature'), Abdulhalim on *My ideal of a leader* ('It is indeed an honour to have the opportunity of giving my opinion'), Tee Chong Swee on *Life for us is better than it was for our forefathers* ('They didn't know that the microbes in the raw food would cause diseases, ladies and gentlemen'), Mahani on the same subject ('Street-lights illuminate our houses and our railway trains are air-conditioned').

All these had a certain charm, even if they had the unintended effect of making me feel like a representative of an ancient, decadent, cynical civilisation. But I remained untouched by Fazmi who talked with owlish seriousness about 'implementing the values of Islam' and spreading the word 'to all the women of Trengganu not to be too revealing, to show the world the morale of the people of Trengganu is not low.' I suppose he meant their morals.

'Cynicism,' I scribbled in the margin of my mark-sheet, 'has yet to be invented here.'

View from a Hill

The town of Kuala Penyu was surrounded on three sides by hills but was itself extremely flat. Everything except the climate made it ideal for cycling, and even the exhausting business of pedalling in the heat must have done a lot towards keeping me fit. I had bought the bicycle (as I told the little girl at the satay stall) from another teacher working for the same company, at a different school. His project was already in its third year, and by now he had advanced to a motorbike.

I realised much later that I had paid Martin an extortionate price for his bicycle, but by the time I came to leave Malaysia I could see exactly what had happened. Every expatriate who takes up his post abroad begins by being rooked. How could it be otherwise, especially in a culture with no concept of the fixed price, and hence of price-tags? The price of anything is as much as some fool can be persuaded to pay. It is also, generally and without any sense of unfairness, higher for the foreigner than the native.

As a result the expatriate, as soon as he has dried off a bit behind the ears, begins to nurse a secret desire to get his own back. When the time comes for his own departure he hunts with smiling, inexorable determination for someone he can rook in his turn. If it is a native of the country, so much the better. However, since almost any inhabitant of the developing world from the age of three upwards has a clearer idea of the value of money than the average British teacher of English, this is unlikely. So who else can he pounce on?

At this moment he realises with a glow of anticipation that (if he is lucky) a kind Providence has seen to it that new teachers arrive in a country, carrying nothing but a couple of suitcases, shortly *before* the old ones finish their contracts. This is his chance. 'Only three hundred for the fridge . . . even if you do buy a car, you'll find a bicycle really useful . . . yes, they're rather nice armchairs, aren't they? . . . you must miss the chance to listen to music if your heavy baggage hasn't arrived yet. I happen to have this stereo cassette-player . . .'

It is all a bit like the depressing law of human nature which dictates that people who were themselves beaten at school tend to grow up wanting to beat other children in their turn. Or, I suppose, remembering my Chinese neighbours, that children who are beaten by their parents tend to look for something defenceless to take it out on, like a kitten.

The best place from which to get an idea of the surrounding geography was from the summit of the headland on the far side of the *kuala*, the river-mouth. To get there you took a ferry and walked through the fishing kampong of Seberang Pintasan, a straggle of wooden houses on stilts lapped by the tidal water. From a distance these looked attractive, shaded by coconut palms and nestled against the steep rocks and windblown woods of the headland. From close to, the effect was spoiled as you became aware of the lack of any rubbish disposal system.

I once took paper, drawing-board and box of pastels across on the ferry, which by now had advanced from sail-power to an outboard motor thanks to a Government grant. I reflected as I climbed the hill that an eighteenth-century English landscape artist, walking through some village in Wiltshire or Westmorland in search of a picturesque or sublime vantage-point, would probably have averted his gaze from the foreground in much the same fastidious way. It was not much of a hill, only a hundred feet or so high, but because it rose sheer from the sea at the end of a long low headland it had a commanding view. In England it would have had a castle built on it hundreds of years ago. Here there was only an unmanned lighthouse.

With that pastel sketch in front of me now, more than four years later, I can feel my way back in imagination to that hilltop above the South China Sea. All sounds are muted by distance (there are no seagulls in Malaysia), and a breeze helps to cool the midday heat. In front of me, beyond a shrub whose young unfolding leaves are a brilliant red, the cliff falls away sheer to a sandy cove inside the harbour-mouth where a blue fishing-boat with a cabin amidships lies beached by the tide. Curving waves lap the crescent of sand behind which the grey stilt-houses shelter from the hot sun, like cattle, beneath a grove of coconut palms.

From down on that beach any view inland would be blocked by the densely forested ridge of hills – two or three hundred feet higher than the one my imagination has perched me on top of – which I found myself staring out at during those first few days in the town, caught in the melancholy of the monsoon, with nowhere to call home except the Kasanya Hotel. From my hilltop I am able to see clear over the base of that rising slope to the bright estuary of the Penyu river receding among the clay-coloured gashes of quarries as far as the irregular humped hills, purple-grey and blurring into the haze, which close the horizon inland.

In that direction there is not much sign of habitation. On the far shore of the estuary, though, the coastal plain extends for several miles as far as a line of peaked hills which close off the bay to the south. Here the town spreads and straggles in an interminable series of kampongs and detached white cement outcrops of speculative development. But from above – once my gaze has travelled past the concrete and wooden buildings of the town centre which line the waterfront – even that urban straggle appears to blend with its surroundings, being so densely planted with coconut palms and the knobbly green humps of fruit trees that all its inland streets seem to blur into one vast plantation. The overflowing rubbish-skips, roaming goats and trickling surface drains are completely lost. So is the Science School, for all its empty acres. Perhaps the State Education Authority was not so niggling after all when it cleared the site.

Imagination glosses over the discomforts. As I was drawing, I remember the sweat dripping from my face on to the picture. Perhaps it helped to fix the powdery pastel, because there is no trace of any mark now. I climbed down the slope towards Seberang Pintasan, pleased with my work, and strolled back through the kampong to the ferry past fallen coconut fronds, grey and weathered and looking like the fallen feathers of some monstrous dinosaurian bird.

The kampong children gathered as I passed. 'Hello . . . hello . . . hello-o . . . *lukis-lukis?* Drawings?'

Sehelai lukis, anyway. One picture, an hour's concentrated work in the sun. I felt drained. John Sell Cotman would have found it tough going in that climate. Or Hokusai, doing all those views of Mount Fuji. No wonder landscape painting seems only to have flourished in the temperate zone.

Further on I passed the old man with the coconut monkey wheeling his bicycle. The monkey was a traditional local answer to the problem of how to get coconuts down from the top of a fifty- or sixty-foot palm tree. Much later I watched operator and monkey at work in another kampong. It was good entertainment on a somnolent afternoon, though I suppose a time-and-motion consultant would have found some room for improvement in the monkey's performance. For every coconut it twisted off and let fall, it must have spent five minutes doing acrobatics among the bases of the fronds. The coconut-monkey-man urged it on with frequent sharp cries while the family which owned the trees sat and watched with relaxed interest. When the monkey had come back down (at amazing speed) its master reeled it in, for all the world like someone reeling in a kite from where it had landed on the grass.

That afternoon at Seberang Pintasan they must have finished their work for the day, because the monkey was perched on the rear rack of the bicycle. Both monkey and owner had a hunched, wary look. I took out my camera.

'*Gambar boleh?* Can I take a picture?'

The old man scowled and stuck out two fingers. Where I come from this is an obscene gesture, but he did not mean it like that. He wanted two dollars for the privilege. I shook my head and walked on, humming to myself, full of the short-lived euphoria of the artist whose latest effort has for once succeeded.

That range of peaked hills which closed off the view along the coast to the south was called Bukit Bauk: Bearded Hill. The highest peak was about fifteen hundred feet high. The range was covered with untouched forest except where a steep narrow tarmac road had been built up to the VHF mast on the summit. I once walked a couple of hundred feet up towards this, but was put off continuing by one of those ominous notices the Malaysian authorities like which say TEMPAT LARANGAN: PROTECTED PLACE and show a graphically stylised representation of a human figure, arms and legs flailing, being shot by someone with a rifle.

To me it seemed the most natural thing in the world to want to climb the highest hill for miles around, but none of the locals thought so. Rosniyah said once in school, almost disapprovingly: 'Peter, we were driving past Bukit Bauk on Saturday and we saw you starting off up the road there. Did you know that was where the local Communists used to meet during the Emergency?' It was as though she were warning me that the place was haunted, not safe to visit even now.

The hills were protected not only by sinister associations and warning signs but by the status of Forest Reserve. The reserve included a large area of more gently hilly country inland from the main range. I once cycled up the side-road which led in this direction, on the way to an isolated hamlet called Jerangau, and stopped by what I thought looked like an attractive vista. Receding perspectives of forest were framed by tall symmetrical trees in the foreground. A disgusting smell stopped me in my tracks, and I realised that I had come upon the festering slopes of the local rubbish tip.

The local people tended to treat the forest rather as the rest of us still persist in treating the sea: as something enormous, limitless, endlessly capable of absorbing the wastes of civilisation. Further on a large rusting car hung almost vertically down the slope, held in place by masses of secondary growth which looked almost as dense as the 'Oasis' foam that flower arrangers use to hold stems in place. The rampant creepers were doing their best to shroud it under a green canopy. Behind it a hillside of massive trees rose undisturbed, for the moment at least.

It was good to see an area of protected primary forest in a country which has recently been so intensively logged, but there was something sad about this particular scene. I wondered how much longer the Bukit Bauk Forest Reserve would last, beleaguered on the one hand by people like my landlord Rasul pushing hard for controls on timber extraction to be loosened, and on the other by people tipping their unwanted household goods into it as though its powers of absorption were infinite.

The Malay word for the secondary scrub which grows up after forest has been cleared, or at least intensively logged, is *belukar*. If you find plants interesting, as I do, you will find plenty to absorb you in the individual species of the *belukar*, which covers a great deal of the Malaysian landscape. On the other hand no-one would claim that this secondary 'forest' looks particularly attractive as a whole. Visually it is simply a tangle of low woodland and scrub which looks oddly nondescript from a distance. The primary (in other words undisturbed) forest on the other hand is extraordinary both in detail and as a whole. Looking from the outside as you approach it you see leaves of every size and shape, from gracefully arching fern-fronds to great incised *tarap* leaves eighteen inches long, with every variation in between. You step through a gap between the intricate leaves, climbing ferns, lianas and buttressed trunks and find yourself within the shrieking stillness of the forest, brown fallen leaves crunching underfoot and the great dipterocarps – the dominant family of forest trees in the region – towering overhead. It is a unique world, as different from a plantation of Sitka spruce – or of rubber trees, for that matter – as something on another planet.

The woody lianas, hanging in twisted loops or zigzags, could look like climbing snakes. Once I came across a real snake coiled up, apparently somnolent, in the tangled lower branches of a bush. It was a handsome creature, rather thickset, with bright beige-and-black patterning dotted with a beautiful silvery-blue. It showed no trace of interest in me, even when I stared at it with bated breath from three feet away, moving slowly backwards. Leafing through a book later I came across its picture and description. It was a Wagler's pit viper, apparently poisonous but unlikely to be deadly. It was the only snake I ever saw in the forest.

One particular part of the reserve not far from the main

road, which at that point started to zigzag in a series of dangerous curves right through it, was my own favourite. It had been designated as the Big Tree Reserve. The big trees were a kind of dipterocarp called *kapor* in Malay. *Kapor* is the same word as 'camphor' in English (I think both come from the same Persian word), and the unwieldy English name is Borneo Camphor-tree. I have never seen the redwoods of California, so for me the dipterocarps of Bukit Bauk remain the ultimate trees, the ones which make tree-worship seem the most innocent and comprehensible of religions.

There were not many of the truly enormous ones, but it was good to see hundreds of well-shaped younger specimens growing beneath and around them. The biggest were about two hundred feet tall, but it was not only their height which was memorable, it was their grace. They had the tall billowing outlines of English elms, but more open and delicate, as though the airy dome of a huge parachute were in the process of separating into scores of small subsidiary domes. Their trunks were slender in proportion to their height. Whether *kapor* flowers have any beauty of colour or scent I have no idea. At that height above the ground they would have been a mystery even if I had been lucky enough to catch one of the infrequent years in which dipterocarps are said to flower. Certainly in that climate there was no question of leaves taking on any vernal or autumnal colour. The beauty of those great trees was linear, or sculptural: elegant outline, straight stem, symmetrical branches. They showed that in rare cases, huge size need not mean a loss of grace. For me they were the single most memorable sight of that part of the East Coast.

No Malaysian I met showed the slightest interest in them, or (with very few exceptions) in any other aspect of the natural world. I began to wonder sometimes if Westerners, particularly the British, were simply a bit dotty on the subject of wildlife. An Indian friend in England once told me of his bafflement when not long after his arrival in London an English colleague had taken him for a walk.

'I thought we were going to see shops, that sort of thing,

but he took me round the park. He showed me different kinds of trees, then he pointed out the birds. I thought he was really strange. Now I've found out a lot of British people are like that. Even in London they like to think they're in the country.'

'It's true, maybe we take it to extremes. But have you never looked at a tree, say, and thought: that's a nice thing to have around?'

He looked almost embarrassed. 'Well . . . I remember once when I was on my way back to India after working in Saudi, and we had to change planes in Karachi. I remember looking down at the trees as we came in to land and thinking: yes, it's nice to see that sort of thing again after the Gulf . . . but I'll tell you one thing I've never understood here, and that's this business of having plants growing inside your houses. Now that I really think is strange.'

Still, if your nature is such that you are more impressed by a two-hundred-foot *kapor* tree than by a two-hundred- (or even eight-hundred-) foot building, you have to go along with what your nature prompts you to feel. I found it hard, for example, to feel equally awed by the development projects being carried out in the state of Selangor, as reported around then in the New Straits Times. The Sultan of Selangor, talking about the gigantic State Mosque on which work had just started at his new capital of Shah Alam, had apparently

> warned 'outsiders' not to question the development projects in Shah Alam, especially the State Mosque. 'I have been told that a group which is unhappy with the construction of the mosque is trying to confuse the people by describing the project as wasteful,' he said today.
>
> The Sultan said Muslims should be proud that Malaysia should be able to build the biggest mosque in Asia. The Sultan also said that while he was abroad recently, he had heard that foreigners were impressed by the fact that the biggest mosque in this region was built in Selangor, a small state.

He hoped that the State Mosque would become the symbol of Islamic supremacy in Selangor and Malaysia.

Looking up at *Dryobalanops aromatica* in the Bukit Bauk Forest Reserve I felt unable to join the Sultan in his megalomaniac piety. I was quite happy to accept those trees as symbols of something or other, though preferably not of Islamic supremacy. Failing that, I was quite happy to accept them as what they were: as some of the most venerable and beautiful organisms on earth, creatures which had taken two or three hundred years to reach that size and deserved every protection the human race could give them and their descendants.

With Malaysia currently (according to mid-1980s figures) the world's largest exporter of tropical timber, it is hard to have much long-term faith in that protection. Like the humpback whale and the white rhinoceros, these forest giants are not safe in our hands. The Western world, having destroyed almost everything it started with, has belatedly woken up to the priority of conserving what little still remains. The developing world still thinks of its resources as infinite. It cannot believe that there will come a time when there is no more forest to gladden the hearts of the timber extractors, no more forest to absorb its junked cars and lorry-loads of refuse. 'Look,' people say, pointing to the forest, 'it's green, it goes on for ever.'

But a few miles on, in the direction of those pointing hands, there are more people. They too are pointing at the trees, and though they do not realise it they are pointing back in the opposite direction. And they are saying the same thing: 'Look, it goes on for ever.'

Long after this I had my first sight of the Selangor State Mosque, then still unfinished, when friends drove me to Shah Alam from their home in Petaling Jaya. Taking off from Subang Airport the following day I had a final view of its huge blue dome as the plane banked. I could not deny that it was impressive. But the domes I still preferred were the green ones at Bukit Bauk.

The hills of that range reached the coast four or five miles south of the town centre, dwindling until at this point only a tump of a wooded hill sixty feet or so high jutted out into the sea. From the end of the beach beside it, not far beyond the Golf Club which marked the furthest tentacle of 'development' in that direction, you could walk through a narrow neck of forest behind this little hill and emerge in the most idyllic bay I have ever seen.

I never found out its real name, so I used to think of it as Robinson Crusoe Bay. It was only a few hundred yards long, a crescent of yellow sand backed by dense forest which rose steeply to the foothills of the Bukit Bauk range, guarded by rocky headlands at either end, with eroded outcrops of brown rock to clamber over at intervals as you walked from one end to the other.

There was no access by road; you had to either climb through the forest or take a boat round the headland. Once I made my way through by the jungle path on a sunny public holiday and was taken aback to find a large Malay family party picnicking on the beach. Otherwise the only people I ever saw there were occasional fishermen who would appear at the rate of one per afternoon, walking slowly from one end to the other to rejoin a boat which was moored round the

next rocky headland. It was the sort of place you could scarcely believe still existed in an age of over-population and intensive tourist development.

If there had been a local cult of swimming or surfing I suppose things would have been very different, but Malays in some ways have a hesitant attitude towards the sea. Often at the end of a fine afternoon you would see families frolicking in the sea near where I lived, with the parents bathing decorously in their sarongs and the children splashing happily, but as far as I could gather people did not 'go swimming' as a recognised activity. I have an idea not many of them ever learned to swim properly. Certainly swimming was an unknown activity at the school, even though its hostels came to within a hundred yards of the beach. Nor did Malays expose their already brown bodies to the hot sun and dazzling reflected light of the beach if they could possibly help it. A sun tan was seen as the very opposite of attractive, and the beauty of a girl was judged at least partly by the fairness of her skin.

In any case, the modesty (or even, by Western standards, prudery) of Muslim attitudes makes Malays reluctant to strip down to anything that might be considered revealing. When Jim, Desmond and I had arrived at the school we had been given an introductory talk by the headmaster; I was about to say an informal talk, but the word would not be accurate as everything in Malay life tends to have a trace of ceremony about it, so that no talk, no meal, no gathering is ever quite informal in the sense we Westerners understand it. He wished us well and passed on various fragments of advice. The one which remained fixed in my memory was the injunction not to wear shorts at any time in the school, even when supervising athletics or coming back in the afternoon for a game of badminton.

'And you must not wear shorts even out of school, when you are in the town. The . . . local people, you see, they have . . . very conservative attitudes.'

He was not a local man himself; he came from the more cosmopolitan West Coast and (rumour had it) chafed at some of the restrictions himself. But he was known to be on the lookout for promotion to an administrative post, and like anyone else in that position he wanted a quiet life with a trouble-free record ('no waves', as the Australians said later), so local customs were allowed to prevail.

The rocky tump like a truncated pyramid which closed off the town side of Robinson Crusoe Bay was covered with trees like a dark wig. Towards the shoreline it reverted to naked ochre rock. The vegetation here, and along the inland edge of the bay where the trees came down to the tideline, was fascinating. There were tall screwpines, or pandanus, like branching palms with hanging fruit which resembled pineapples. There were cycads a few feet high, one of the most ancient and curious plant-families on earth, something between a short-trunked palm and a tree-fern in appearance, but in the evolutionary sense quite distinct from either. From the trees which jutted out over the rocky promontory at the end of the bay dangled festoons of a creeper with curiously thick oval leaves. It was not until I saw this bearing its little pinky-red flowers, so artificial-looking it was as if someone had hooked them in place on the hanging stems, that I recognised it as *Hoya*, the wax-flower I remembered my mother growing as a house-plant years before. That one had grown tightly round a metal hoop in the shelter of the front porch, but its wild cousins here dangled twenty feet from the branches overhead.

Sitting perched on the rocky headland above the beach, with bead curtains of *Hoya* foliage to one side and a spreading branch sheltering me from the brilliant sun, I could see hordes of small crabs perching on the limpet-covered rocks beneath with the tide lapping their shells. Mudskippers three or four inches long with frog-like eyes flickered over the surface of the miniature bays between the rocks, hopping out now and then to sun themselves just above the tideline, heads upwards, like Galapagos iguanas in miniature. Higher up, out of reach of the slapping waves, were odd little scurrying creatures like a cross between woodlice and tiny shrimps.

VIEW FROM A HILL

The other side of the headland, on my way from the town, I had come across a king crab, or horseshoe crab, a strange shiny-shelled creature with a body about a foot long and a projecting spike of a tail. The shell looked as though it were made of plastic, a dull bottle-green in colour. It was in sections, shallowly domed, so that the creature was streamlined into the sand like a miniature tank in the desert. Underneath, entirely concealed, it had twelve or fourteen legs in two groups. There was very little else under that hollow domed shell, so that you wondered where the creature found room for its vital organs.

With its apparently plastic shell and mechanical-looking innards it looked like some man-made device out of a science-fiction story. In fact, like the cycads growing on the rock-ledge to one side, it was a prehistoric creature: not a crab at all, despite its name, but the closest living relative of the trilobites of the Silurian oceans.

Someone had overturned it when I found it, exposing its uncompromising inner machinery. I turned it back the right way up before I waded across the mouth of a lagoon to the start of the forest path. When I came back several hours later it had moved round in a small circle, scoring a shallow track in the sand. I did not know whether it was making its way towards the sea or looking for somewhere to lay its eggs, like a turtle, so I left it alone.

The first time I went to the bay, to swim and explore and revel in the clean brilliant sunlight, I was overtaken by the weather on the way home. It had been dazzlingly sunny all day, but around three in the afternoon magnificent black clouds began to spread from inland, leaving a mysterious streak of yellow light above the seaward horizon. As I trudged back along the beach, the heavens opened. Out to sea it was still clear, with marvellously intricate patterns on the surface of the water. The effect was unnaturally clear and three-dimensional, like something seen under an electron microscope, with every kind of reticulation and ribbing and pock-marking on a burnished monochrome surface like some precious metal. The twin-peaked summit of Pulau

Tinggol, the local offshore island, stood out dark against the sky. There were a few fishing boats visible. I was glad I was not out with them. It struck me as an afternoon for being ashore, with a home to go back to.

I trudged on in the warm deluging rain, trying to navigate my way across the firm stretches of sand, half-hypnotised by the effects created by that low eerie light on the disturbed water, wondering vaguely how I was going to manage a painting of Robinson Crusoe Bay.

A later visit was less idyllic. I had decided to climb up the slope at the far end of the bay to find out what lay beyond. It was the sort of place which fills you with a childish curiosity, as though you were back on a seaside holiday at the age of nine looking for the chance to go exploring. I wanted to know if there were further bays to discover or nothing but a massive headland with no further access to the sea for miles.

The slope was a gentle one, covered with low scrub as opposed to dense forest. It looked feasible. I scrambled for five minutes between thorny screwpines, tussocks of long coarse grass and outcrops of rock, wondering obscurely whether it was the kind of terrain which snakes liked, when I became aware of some kind of large insect flying nearby.

After that everything happened with amazing rapidity. Something was trapped in my hair, and I was dizzy with pain and shock. Something else was attacking my arm. I staggered back down the slope, arms flailing, losing a sandal in the process and risking a broken ankle at every stumbling step. All I could manage to glimpse of the creatures which were attacking me was that they were huge and black and buzzed like bees, which is what I suppose they must have been. If they really were bees they were enormous ones. Back in England, staying with market-gardening friends, I had once manoeuvred a swarm of bees from the branch of a tree into a cardboard box, wearing a bee-keeper's hat and veil and gloves. The one sting I got in the process was nothing to these. My arm was still swollen a week afterwards.

I raced across the narrow strip of beach and ended up

lying on my face in the shallows of the sea, splashing water over my head. When I got up, a little unsteadily, the bees had gone. I had one sting on the forearm, one on the shoulder, one on my left ear and one (the most painful by far) on the top of my head, which felt as though a band of red-hot iron were tied tightly round it. I made my way back along the beach and through the forest path to where I had left my bicycle at the Golf Club, then with a final effort cycled the three miles to some friends with a house along the beach who gave me aspirin and anti-histamine and ran me the final mile home in their car. It was another re-run of 'The Lion's Mane'.

I never did find out what lay beyond that far headland. On my mental map of the area it is tentatively marked 'Forbidden Bay', and beside this is written in Gothic letters HERE BE BEASTIES.

I called it Robinson Crusoe Bay simply because it seemed to fit the part more perfectly than any other stretch of coast I had ever seen. There are other contenders, of course, including some of the local offshore islands which I was to visit later, and there must be many worse winter parlour games than arguing over the merits of different ones. It also happened that every time I went there I was on my own, so I suppose it was natural enough that I should associate that secluded stretch of coast with a certain amount of solitary brooding.

There may be a basic inclination in the human heart, or soul, to want to climb up to somewhere high – even the smallest hilltop will do – when it is unhappy. It is not only aspiring suicides who seek out high places to brood in. I have a clear memory of sitting on that little rocky tump of a headland beneath the tangled clump of trees which huddled together on top of it like a group of picnickers stranded by the tide, watching the waves prostrating themselves on the beach beneath, and feeling acutely miserable. This feeling was not improved when I got up to leave and found myself sliding down the slope faster than I had intended, while wearing nothing but a pair of swimming trunks. As I probably knew in a vague theoretical way at the time, the human buttocks are not adapted for use as a brake.

It seems an appropriately bathetic note on which to add that the reason I was brooding was that a love-affair had come to an end, and my heart felt almost as painful as my backside.

RAIN-FOREST

Green has no power
To drive thoughts away,
Nor can hue of flower
Or shape of leaf
Give relief:
The same cares stay.

The forest endlessly
Repeats its theme;
Each leaf, each tree
Can do no more
Than underscore
The general scheme

Whose web, whose sullen net
So traps the eye
It cannot stir to let
The grieving mind
Look up and find
The open sky.

PART TWO

Country Music at the Federal

If you assemble a crowd of total strangers in a luxury hotel (taking care to choose a country, perhaps even a continent, which very few of them have ever visited before), accommodate them two to a room and keep them there for something over three weeks, you are (at the very least) taking risks with human behaviour. It is a potentially explosive situation, particularly when the people concerned know that at the end of those three weeks they are going to be sent to strange towns, perhaps hundreds of miles away from what soon comes to feel like a reassuring home base, and left to get on with a job which with each passing day of lectures comes to sound even more demanding.

From a management point of view, of course, it may be a very good way of finding out in advance which of the new entrants are likely to start breaking under stress. But that only helps to prove my point.

In fact it is just the kind of hothouse situation English detective writers of the so-called Golden Age liked to start with. If Agatha Christie or Ngaio Marsh had lived until the era of contract English language teaching abroad, they might have seized on it avidly. Ten little TEFL teachers? Murder in Malaysia? The whole situation, it seemed to me sometimes, was very like being on a cruise liner, which is itself a favourite detective-story setting. You had the same basic ingredients: the enclosed world, which forces people into each other's company more quickly and more intensively than anything they would come across in the normal run of things; the novel situation, with those hints of the exotic which loosen people's inhibitions with such depressing predictability; the business of being uprooted from familiar points of reference, which makes even normally self-reliant people look for someone else to cling to.

And lastly, the element of obvious luxury which gives an air of unreality to things, as though you are in a world of pure artifice where moments of play-acting come to seem as real as anything else, a stage-set full of the vulgar trappings of Romance. Or to put it more cynically, a series of disasters waiting to happen.

'The personalities of the members of the group' (I wrote in my journal quite early on, with an admirable philosophical poise I was not fated to maintain for long) 'are getting more definite. I suppose as the initial novelty of the physical surroundings begins to wear off, so you develop a better eye for human personalities.' There was Cyril Boldwood, for example, a trim, highly organised man a couple of years older than myself who had been teaching English in the Air Force of one of the Gulf countries. I gathered that he was recently divorced. There was Mungo McKechnie, an affable, melancholy, indecisive West Highlander who had already been in Malaysia for three years and was transferring to this new project.

Then there was Stuart Robertson, a thickset red-haired bristly little man who spoke (despite his Scottish name) in an impeccable but almost totally inaudible Oxford accent. He had been teaching in various parts of tropical Asia and perhaps elsewhere; it was hard to know how much of what he said about himself to believe. Despite the fact that he talked almost without pausing for breath, I would catch very little of his monologue (perhaps mercifully) because his chief concern seemed to be to inform his bristly beard what a remarkably accomplished person he was.

'And then,' he would say as I nodded in vague unwilling encouragement, 'I was asked – specially asked, mind you – to run a special mmbl mmbl mmhm for the mmbhm mmbhm . . . you see I was the only person there who knew how to mblmbl . . . they begged me not to go but I said . . . mmhm . . . MA in Applied Linguistics . . . mmhm . . . mblbl . . . organised a series of lectures . . . mblbl . . .'

'Mm,' I would say, getting caught up in the spirit of the

thing. And Stuart's red beard would bristle proudly, hearing the marvellous things its master had done and which it alone was privileged to hear about.

There was Desmond whom I shared a room with. Then there were twenty-five or so other people I got to know more slowly, or not at all. And then there was Fiona, who was tall and dark and lithe, classically beautiful rather than merely pretty, who had the temperament of a fire-goddess from some world of untamed mythology. I found her breathtaking and disconcerting by turns. Of all those 'personalities of the group' who were in my mind when I scribbled that journal entry, hers was the one I was most vividly aware of.

The course of lectures and 'workshop' sessions (they would have sounded more entertaining if spelled, Malay phonetic English style, as WOKSYOP) was nothing if not intensive. We lurched with barely a break from *Cultural expectations in Malaysian society* to *A simplified syllabus for Form I teaching*. After something like a solid week of this we had the luxury of a weekend off. The cruise liner had called into port; we had a day and a half in which to see the sights. As we left the last session of the week the plaintive voice of one of the organisers could be heard calling out: 'I have a few spare copies of the leaflet on self-directed learning if anyone would like one . . .' Nobody looked back.

Fiona, Cyril and I took a bus out to Batu Caves, a few miles out of the city, for the Saturday afternoon. We clambered up an apparently endless flight of steps to the caves, which are set in one of a series of huge limestone outcrops which thrust out of the landscape near the northern boundaries of Kuala Lumpur. Grey macaque monkeys scrambled up the lianas which hung in front of the rock-face as we ascended. They managed to climb a great deal faster than we did. At the top we found ourselves standing in something like a cathedral which had partly melted.

Batu Caves are very much an Indian area, the starting-point for the Thaipusam devotional festival which was coming up soon. In a subsidiary cave was something like an art gallery of Hindu deities in the form of life-size figurines illuminated by coloured lights. One god danced on a many-spoked wheel. A moustachioed naked dwarf like a cherub which had mysteriously reached the age of puberty clutched a snake, apparently untroubled by the fact that he was being trampled underfoot. In a sort of celestial maternity ward an array of male babies sprawled on lotus-flowers while a benevolent goddess looked on.

There was a large book in my mother's bookshelf when I was a child called *Indian Myth and Legend*. It must have dated from around 1920. I used to leaf through it in fascination, my imagination caught by the strange names and the numerous black-and-white photographic plates of Hindu gods from blackened and broken temple bas-reliefs. I found them fascinating and at the same time obscurely nightmarish. These South Indian figurines, on the other hand, were jolly and colourful and rather endearing.

The following evening Fiona telephoned my room to say that she and a small group of other people were going to eat at a restaurant not far away. Would I like to come? I joined the group, which included Cyril, Mungo and a woman called Muriel who had been assigned to share a room with Fiona.

There were about thirty people in our particular intake, but comparatively few of them were women and of those, very few indeed were unattached. I add this statistical note in case it helps to explain some of the increasingly bizarre events which followed. Fiona was one of the few unattached ones. Muriel was another, so it was logical of the company to put them in the same room even though they had little else in common.

Muriel was around fifty, older than any of the rest of the group except one man who might have had a couple of years on her. I think she was (naturally enough) rather conscious of the fact. She was intelligent in an academic sort of way and odd in most other respects: a prim, awkward, slightly hard-to-handle middle-aged spinster with a monotonous voice. Like Desmond and Stuart in their different ways she seemed to lack whatever essential fitment it is that enables human beings to make easy social contact with each other. She was hard work to be with, like some difficult aunt remembered from childhood.

I thought in passing as we sat in the flickering candlelight of the restaurant that she was exactly the sort of character you meet early on in one of those Agatha Christie or Ngaio Marsh detective stories and know intuitively will be the first murder victim, probably somewhere near the end of the third chapter. All of which is probably grossly unfair to poor Muriel, but people without that easy sociable side to their natures – the people who go through life giving the impression that they have always just missed everyone else – seem to be fated to have unfair things said about them. It is almost as though they invited it.

I had picked up several points about Fiona by now. I knew, for example, that she hated smoking and also fireworks, because I had seen how disconcerted she was by the firecrackers exploding in the city streets in anticipation of Chinese New Year, so what followed was doubly unfortunate. After the main course Cyril was lighting a cigar at the candle-flame when suddenly, without warning, he started waving a lighted sparkler round his head. He must have lit it behind his back without anyone noticing. The room filled with a choking sulphurous smoke. Everyone in the group stopped eating and stared, open-mouthed.

Fiona said in her clear voice with its trace of Edinburgh accent: 'Cyril, that was a very *stupid childish* thing to do.' The rest of us looked on blankly, our faces melodramatically lit by the candles and the rain of sparks, our reactions dulled by several glasses of wine.

Cyril, puffing away at his cigar, quite unruffled, with the light gleaming on his glasses, had the air of a plutocrat from a thirties caricature. The sparkler – it was some special kind made for Chinese New Year – went on burning for what seemed an inordinately long time. He looked aside at it, his poise briefly weakening. It must have come over him that this was one of those gestures which seem a good idea at the time but fail to catch on. With a quick decisive movement he dipped the sparkler into his glass of water like a swizzle-stick.

The sparkler, unperturbed, went on flaring brightly. A cloud of steam, blending with the sulphurous smoke and the effusions of his cigar, gathered above the glass. Half-lost in the middle of this thickening miasma, Cyril managed to retain most of his poise, like an aristocratic comedian getting the cold shoulder while doing the Northern circuit, but refusing to be fazed by it. I admired him. Lesser men would have dissolved into a puddle of humiliation under the table.

I heard Fiona muttering in exasperation. 'How many coffee?' a voice repeated several times into my ear. It was the Chinese waitress. Her eyes had the unconcerned look of someone who had seen worse in her time. It was some while before she managed to get a coherent order.

Eventually the sparkler went out, and there was a heavy silence. We had had either too much or too little to drink. We should by rights have been prostrate with hysterical laughter, but perhaps the volume, or mileage, or acreage, of lectures we had endured in the course of the previous week had numbed our sense of the ridiculous. The meal had gone flat, like the only attempt at a cake I have ever baked: all the currants in a soggy mass at the bottom and apparently no way of stirring them up to the top again. I groped for a currant or two, but failed.

Next to me Muriel was talking in her precise, slightly sing-song voice about the palmy days of the late sixties: protests in Grosvenor Square, the barricades in Paris. I sipped coffee, trying to remember where I was and what I was supposed to be doing there. There was probably a perfectly obvious answer; it was just very difficult to imagine what it could possibly be.

'It was the year the lesbians came out. I remember it quite clearly.'

I woke from my trance with a jerk. 'What?'

'Sixty-nine,' said Muriel dreamily, 'the year the lesbians came out.'

It seemed to me that it was time to go back home. Which

for the moment, in the absence of anything better, meant the Federal Hotel.

When we got back, the country-and-western band (country-and-eastern, somebody had nicknamed it) was playing in the hotel bar, which went under the name of the Western Saloon. There were four of them, cheerful Portuguese Eurasians from Malacca. They called themselves *Os Pombos*: The Pigeons. Mungo was a great fan of theirs. His wife had recently left him, so it may be that the plangent foursquare platitudes of the music, with its note of amplified self-pity, were exactly what he needed.

I found later that a cup of local coffee made with condensed milk, taken half-way through the morning at school, had a similar pick-me-up effect on my own system. It was not a nice drink in itself, too sickly-sweet for comfort, but you could feel it doing your metabolism good. So (I suppose) with Mungo and the country-and-western songs.

There was a football tournament on in the city at the time, and teams from Brazil and Swansea were staying at the hotel. Swansea as it happened were Muriel's home team, and we left her happily in pursuit of autographs. Mungo, Fiona and I went into the bar and exchanged long-suffering glances, then sat down with Coke and beer to enjoy the spectacle of the gold-digging girls who had been waiting expectantly by the door being escorted off to dance with off-duty footballers from South Wales.

The Eurasian band, ten-gallon hats and all, sang something about the road to Texarkana. Mungo settled back comfortably in his chair and raised his glass mug of Anchor beer.

'Aye,' he said dreamily, 'the boys are guid. D'ye not think so, Fiona?'

And so ended my first week in the bazaars and byways of the mysterious East.

There followed another week of wading shoulder-deep through lectures. Malay culture. Chinese culture. Islam. Life in a Malaysian town. Malay for beginners. Schemes of work. Listening skills. During an afternoon's break from all this Fiona and I went for a long walk round the city, a forest of skyscrapers littered with remnants of Chinatown. It seemed a relatively cheerful place; when I learned more of its history I found it hard to realise that in May 1969 a single night of race rioting (provoked by an unexpected election result) had left two hundred people shot or hacked to death in the street, according to official accounts, or according to unofficial ones more like two thousand.

'A Chinese corpse hanging from every lamp-post between the Padang and the airport,' said an Englishman I met later in Sri Lanka. There is no way of arriving at an accurate total since Malaysians, for obvious reasons, do not talk much about their Kristallnacht. Race relations between Malays and Chinese present the visitor with no obvious signs of festering. There are no sullen ghettoes, no gangs of teenagers out for trouble. 'They're giving us an object lesson in how it all ought to be done,' says the visitor, impressed by the sight of Mr Lim and Mr Velu and Encik Hamid eating *laksa* together at a Malay foodstall. But when Kuala Lumpur or Jakarta explodes, the result makes the Notting Hill or Brixton riots look like a disorganised children's party.

It is why the Malaysian government seems so paranoid to Westerners, why instead of letting little puffs of steam escape from time to time to lower the pressure, they seal every vent in the machinery with the Internal Security Act and the full Asian paraphernalia of total enforced radio silence. Of course there are some small social problems in our country, the official line runs, all of them (needless to say) inherited from years of colonial misrule, but aside from those all is for the best in the best of all possible developing worlds.

There are subjects in Malaysia which its citizens are literally forbidden to talk about under threat of instant arrest and detention: race relations, for example, or the dominant position of the Malays vis-à-vis other races in the Government or the armed forces; the position of the monarchy (which is absolute and not subject to the law in any way); the position of Islam as the official religion. The Sultan of Selangor, in the New Straits Times article I quoted earlier, was happy with the praise of 'foreigners' from outside Malaysia. But the 'outsiders' he was warning to stay silent were Malaysians: the non-Muslim fifty per cent of the country's population who might reasonably query the use of their own hard-earned taxes to construct the biggest mosque in Asia, for no better reason than to assert the supremacy of Islam in the region.

In London race relations are in all obvious ways worse, or at least more distrustful and embittered, than anything in Kuala Lumpur. And yet Londoners do not fear the kind of explosion of hatred and screaming, *parang*-waving, blood-letting vengeance which haunts the minds of those who remember May 1969 in Malaysia. This includes a number of people in pastel-coloured, hi-tech, squeaky-clean Singapore, that model Asian state across the causeway from scruffy Johore Bahru. To run amuck – *amok* – is a Malay expression. To an outsider there is an inescapable connection between the blind outburst of indiscriminate violence which the word implies and the Government's total, carefully-policed clampdown on any form of discussion or debate. The two extremes are more closely related to one another than either is to any 'middle ground'.

In American terms, people do not let it all hang out in East Asia. It is a subcontinent of emotions so carefully buttoned-down it makes the middle-class English seem as laid-back as Californians.

I once helped to coach the school's English-language debating team for a national inter-school competition. We worked by preparing all twenty or so of the previously-circulated list of topics. One of the last ones on the list was: *Money is the most powerful human driving force of all.*

Various ideas came up. No, we said, what about family, love, ambition for power, patriotism, revenge?

'And religion,' I said. 'That's been a pretty powerful driving force all through history.'

There was a silence. My Indian colleague Navamalar (who was in charge) and the four wimpled Malay girls who made up the team looked at each other.

'Look at the Crusades,' I said, warming to my theme. 'Or the lives of the Prophets. Muslims and Christians. The Buddha. Saints. Great leaders. Mystics. Muhammad Ali Jinnah. John Wesley . . .'

There was a faint sound of papers and feet being shuffled. I became aware that everybody was looking somewhere else.

'Well? Don't you agree?'

Navam cleared her throat and said delicately: 'Probably you are right, but you see, we can't include that.'

'Why on earth not?'

'It's a sensitive subject. Religion, you see . . . we simply don't dare mention it. The team would lose marks, perhaps be disqualified.'

'Sensitive subjects' are clearly specified in Malaysia. In English pubs, people are traditionally enjoined to steer clear of two topics: politics and religion. In Malaysia the ban covers the whole of society, and it is not a half-joking caveat but an injunction backed by the full force of law. Behind it, like a nightmare which has receded but refuses quite to fade, is the memory of May 1969.

At the time I knew nothing of this. All I knew was that the population of the country was mixed, that about half was Malay and a third Chinese, eked out with so-called Indians (mostly in fact of Sri Lankan Tamil descent, like Navamalar, but including Malayalis from Kerala and Sikhs and Singhalese and all sorts) and the various Borneo tribes of Sarawak and Sabah: Iban, Kadazan, Murut, Bidayuh, Kayan, Kelabit, Bajau and all the rest. I liked the human variety of the streets, as most visitors do. It is rarely foreigners who object to the presence of immigrants in a country.

Fiona and I walked along what under the British was called Batu Road (it leads ultimately to Batu Caves) but has since been named Jalan (i.e. Road or Street) Tunku Abdul Rahman. I would be the last person to wish to deny that civilised, courageous and amusing old man the honour of having the city's central shopping street named after him, but it does mean that people end up calling it 'Jalan TAR'.

Malaysians love long names, and at the same time, perversely, love reducing them to initials. I held back for a long time from referring to Kuala Lumpur as 'KL' in the belief that it was some kind of arrogant colonial vestige, but in fact Malaysians themselves use the abbreviation just as much. It extends to other towns too. Johore Bahru is JB, Kuala Trengganu is KT, Kota Kinabalu is KK, unless you are in Perak, where KK means Kuala Kangsar.

It is not an efficient system of nicknames. A friend working in the state of Johore frowned in puzzlement when I talked about flying to KT. 'But there isn't an airport at Kota Tinggi,' he said. People in Brunei have what seems a heretical tendency to refer to Kuala Belait, the country's second town, as KB, when every Malaysian knows that KB is really Kota Bahru. On the other hand Kuala Baram in Sarawak, only a few miles across the border from Kuala Belait, is always referred to by its full name. Two KBs in twenty miles or so would be too much for even Malaysians to handle.

Even a new housing estate can end up being christened something like Taman (i.e. park or garden) Tun Syed Dr Mohammed Ismail. In the small English town I grew up in there are two adjacent roads in a council estate which dates from the sixties: Winston Road and Churchill Road. The combination of off-hand brevity and economy would be impossible in Malaysia, where there would have to be a single road called something like Jalan Sir Winston son of Lord Randolph. And of course if the dignitary in question has made the pilgrimage to Mecca there is no way of omitting *Haji* from the name.

The company I worked for entered whole-heartedly into the spirit of things with its Regional Project Directors and Orientation Courses. You heard fragments of dialogue out of a Peter Cook and Dudley Moore sketch:

'Why haven't we seen the RPD lately? I thought he was bringing us those OHTs.'

'He's in KL organising an OC. Then he's off to UK to do an MA in TEFL.'

Not everyone speaks the same language of abbreviations, which makes for further pitfalls, or pratfalls. I once overheard a conversation between Jim and Desmond at the school canteen. Jim was talking about the problems of getting a cheap flight to the UK which would not run the risk of either being cancelled because of mechanical failure or leaving him stranded for an unscheduled week in Moscow because of Aeroflot. I should explain that the Malaysian national carrier is called MAS (Malaysian Airlines System, though *mas* also conveniently happens to mean 'gold' in Malay: 'we'll treat you like gold,' say the advertisements). Cynics say the letters stand for *mana ada sistem* which means 'Where's the system'?

'It's all very well flying MAS,' said Jim, 'but the trouble with them is that they only have two Jumbos, and what happens if one of them goes u/s?'

'But they don't fly there,' said Desmond with perfect seriousness.

The award for the longest set of initials in the Malay world should go to a headmaster I knew in the Sultanate of Brunei, where titles are abundant and interminable. The Headmaster was a *Pengiran*, a title roughly equivalent to Prince but devalued by overabundance. I was puzzled by the fact that every document which issued from his office said at the bottom left-hand corner PHDBPHP/JH. JH was obviously the secretary, but what were the other letters? Perhaps it was one of those old signing-off flourishes like SWALK for Sealed With A Loving Kiss. *Patient, Hopeful, Dedicated: Be Pure-Hearted. Peter.* Or *Philip: Help Dad Buy Present – Hardy Perennials?* Or *Please Hose Down Both Parts of the Houses of Parliament*.

Belatedly I realised that they must be the Pengiran's initials. His name, which I had never fully registered, turned out to be Pengiran Haji Daud bin Pengiran Haji Puteh. In conversation he seemed a modest unassuming man, inclined to be self-conscious because his English was not as fluent as he would have liked.

At the metropolitan end of Jalan Tunku Abdul Rahman,

alias Jalan TAR, alias Batu Road, the cityscape opens out to reveal its historic heart: the Padang, a large rectangular green. Not far away is the original 'muddy confluence' of two rivers which gave the city its Malay name. Fiona and I went into the little Anglican church at one end of the Padang and felt a mild cultural disorientation (literally: a state of no longer being aligned towards the East) in this white Church of England interior with its unexpected ceiling fans. The stained-glass windows commemorate the planters murdered during the so-called Emergency (which was really a fully-fledged civil war) during the fifties. From here we walked on past various imposing, in some cases very elegant, skyscrapers to the Railway Station. The British, in a rare moment of imagination free from nostalgia, built this in a spectacular Muslim Eastern style with turreted cupolas and pillared arcades like something from Mogul India.

It was a sunny afternoon, and by now we were dehydrated. In the station restaurant I chose something in a dispenser which I took to be Coke, but which turned out to be a concoction called root beer. I learned later that this had become enormously popular in Malaysia, where people like their drinks sickly-sweet: so popular that it even has its own Malay phonetic spelling: *Rut Bir*. It tasted like Euthymol toothpaste dissolved in turpentine. It seemed to me one of the nastiest drinks I had ever tasted, nastier even than the stuff they sell in Peru under the name of Inca-Cola, which is saying something. I was so thirsty that I drank it before stopping to grumble about it.

That night the hotel room which Fiona shared with Muriel was broken into. Cyril, Desmond and I rushed up when Fiona told us, to find suitcases emptied and their contents strewn all over the floor. Some money was missing.

Cyril took the situation in at a glance, but misread it. Muriel was out being comforted by friends. Fiona was standing looking at the wreckage in what he took to be a state of shocked dismay, but which I suspected (rightly as it turned out) to be mounting indignation. She was not a girl I ever saw reduced to total helplessness. Cyril seemed to take an invisible clip-board from under his arm as he bent towards her. It was as if he had looked up the appropriate page in an Air Force Manual: *Women, hysterical, what to do in the case of*.

'Shall I ask for some food to be sent up, Fiona?'

Fiona's indignation surged up like a waterspout. Her eyes flashed. She was every inch the fiery Highland girl.

'Oh, Cyril, for GOD'S SAKE!'

Cyril crossed out a few lines on that page of his invisible Air Force manual. Obviously the section needed updating. He looked at her with a faint frown, waiting for her to subside into a more manageable pattern of behaviour. It was quite obvious that he wanted to fuss over her, and equally obvious that anything resembling fussing was liable to provoke a further outburst.

Desmond, for once, rose to the occasion. 'Don't think she really wants us here,' he said, his eyes flickering evasively towards the far wall. 'Come on.'

I looked at him with gratitude as he left the room with Cyril reluctantly in tow. I was left on my own with Fiona to provide un-fussy reassurance.

When the waterspout had subsided a very small smiling man arrived to find out what had happened. Fiona and I took him to be a security guard, but she discovered the next day that he was a car park attendant. Later he was followed by a large, jovial, ineffectual-looking police sergeant. Side by side they had the air of a classic comedy team. Something told me Fiona was unlikely to get her money back.

'Er . . . *Tuan Inspektor* . . .'

He smiled deprecatingly. '*Sarjan* only,' he said, but he did not look displeased.

He handed Fiona a report form to be completed in duplicate while he and the car park attendant engaged me in polite conversation. I noticed with a certain unease (bearing in mind Fiona's volcanic nature) that they addressed almost all their remarks to me, not her. I suppose it must have seemed perfectly clear to them. Here was the helpful reliable male colleague taking charge of the difficult situation while the frail female sat at the dressing-table calming her fluttering heart by filling in a form in duplicate: *Nama penuh dalam huruf besar*: FIONA GILLESPIE CAMERON. *Pekerjaan*: Teacher. Coming on top of Cyril's unwanted solicitude it was the Little Woman syndrome with a vengeance. I looked aside and saw her reflected in the dressing-table mirror, quivering with nerves and indignation as she wrote.

The tireless officials, having examined possible points of entry and muttered darkly about foreign football teams, took themselves off not long before midnight. A helpful lady from the company brought us each an enormous gin-and-tonic, which tasted like nectar, and Room Service sent up chicken sandwiches with compliments of the hotel. Cyril's instincts had been right; it was just his timing which had been out by about four hours.

'That Desmond, you know,' said Fiona as she finished the last of her gin. 'I don't know why you complain about him. At least he knows when to keep his mouth shut.'

By now it was almost time for us to leave Kuala Lumpur: to 'go out-station', as it was still sometimes quaintly phrased. The postings had been arranged, not without some acrimony, late in the course. The town Jim, Desmond and I had been posted to was six hours' drive away: four hours across the peninsula via Temerloh, then a final run up the coast from Kuantan where Mungo, Fiona and Stuart had been posted. In Mungo's case it was by prior arrangement because he had already been working at another school in the town for three years and was still renting a house there. It was a monstrous palace with five bedrooms, and now that his wife had left him he obviously felt the need for company. He offered hospitality to Fiona and Stuart until they found houses of their own.

This sounded a better deal than staying for days on end at some poky hotel on the lines of the Kasanya (a pleasure which was still in store for me at the time), and they were both glad to accept. We arranged for a fleet of share-taxis at nine in the morning (there were boxes of school-books to carry, provided by the company, as well as our own luggage), went out in a group for a North Indian meal at the glittering Shiraz restaurant and returned to the Western Saloon for a final drink.

Everything, in other words, was working out fairly efficiently, and there was plenty of goodwill in the air. The girls sipped cocktails, the men gin or beer. Os Pombos sang "Whah dew yew treat muh lahk yew dew?" It was all too good to last. Stuart, who had not been at the Shiraz, arrived at the bar late and was told about the morning's travel arrangements. They were not what he had had in mind. He puffed out his chest like a pouter pigeon, bristling at every follicle.

'This is impossible! I can't possibly go along with that. Nobody asked me. I don't want to leave till eleven, as it happens. I don't expect to have to agree to things without being consulted.'

At this point Fiona and I went to the bar to pay for a round of drinks and missed an escalation of hostilities. We came back in time to see Mungo, smouldering, being held back bodily. He was not a big man, but at the moment he looked menacing. With his private life in the state it was, he was obviously in no mood to suffer fools gladly. A kind of clan warfare seemed on the point of erupting. It was as though the country-and-western band had started to play a pibroch.

'Nobody talks to me like that and gets away with it, d'ye hear me?'

Stuart, his red stubble of beard bristling in solidarity with his injured dignity, stood there like a squat fighting cock. His voice for once had passed the threshold of audibility.

'You can't intimidate me, you know! People can't simply expect to make arrangements for other people as though they were pieces of luggage or something . . .'

'And you can forget what I said about offering you hospitality. You'll not be coming into my house, Stuart Robertson. And that's my last word on the subject.'

'I'd rather stay in a hotel anyway.'

'And so you shall, my wee mannie, so you shall. If any o' them'll have you.'

People hauled them away in different directions. Fiona came back after having a word with Mungo. She glared fiercely in the direction of Stuart, who was on his way out of the bar by now, radiating indignation at every bristle.

'That man really is the most pompous, poisonous little . . .'

It looked as if our departure was not going to be quite so jolly after all. Staff-room life at the Science School, Kuantan, looked as if it might have its tense moments.

'Listen,' said Fiona. 'It's just possible I may be walking into a madhouse. Phone me as soon as you've found somewhere to live. You've got Mungo's number. I'll come up and see you during Chinese New Year.'

When I talk about Kuala Penyu being six hours' drive away from the capital, I mean six hours in a share-taxi. The share-taxi system is not unique to West Malaysia, but it must be as highly developed there as anywhere in the world. Each town, however small, has a 'taxi-stand' somewhere near the centre. If the town is big enough, there are different departure bays for different destinations. You merely wait for three other like-minded people to turn up, and you are off. The taxis are usually Mercedes diesels. A full taxi takes four passengers, but if you are in a hurry you can charter the whole car. Or if only two other people have turned up and you are tired of waiting, you can pay for two seats.

It is not an expensive way to travel, even so. During my time in the country an entire taxi – four times the single fare – from Kuantan to Kuala Penyu cost about as much as a British Rail ticket from Liverpool Street to Ipswich, a roughly equivalent distance.

The only catch is the standard of driving, which (as even Malaysians themselves admit) tends to be atrocious. The taxi-drivers generally adopt what I cannot help thinking of as the Muslim style of driving. This involves travelling at top speed, without any particular aggressiveness of the Western *macho* variety but with no concern for safety whatever and a blind faith in God. Newcomers to the share-taxi system travel whole journeys at a stretch with their eyes tightly closed and their fingernails needing to be surgically extracted from their palms afterwards.

There are sources of passing unease quite apart from considerations of road safety. Mungo and I (he was the 'co-ordinator' for his group of teachers, as I was for mine) once shared a taxi on our way back to the East Coast after a conference in the capital. We had the back seat to ourselves: three seats paid between two. In the front seat was a middle-aged Chinese lady. The driver was an excitable, twitching Malay wearing the *peci*, the white skull-cap which shows that the wearer has made the *haj*, the pilgrimage to Mecca. If I were a Muslim I suppose this would have given me unbounded faith in the driver's sanctity, but I am not a Muslim. If anything, it seemed to me that the Hajis drove even worse than anyone else. Perhaps having made their spiritual pilgrimage they felt themselves to be above mundane considerations like road safety.

The first part of the drive from Kuala Lumpur to Kuantan takes you through some impressive scenery as the Karak Highway (notorious for its accident rate and its landslides) zigzags up out of the lowlands. On this particular journey it was impossible to relax and enjoy the view. Mungo and I exchanged uneasy glances as the driver, twitching and muttering to himself as though he were listening to Michael Jackson on an invisible Walkman, grabbed an aerosol can of air-freshener and repeatedly sprayed the lap of the Chinese woman next to him. Now and then, for good measure, he aimed the can haphazardly over his shoulder and directed a jet of choking perfume back at us.

Jigging convulsively as the taxi swerved round a corner with a crumbling cliff-face hanging over us on one side and a five-hundred-foot slope falling away on the other, he fished a plastic inhaler from his shirt pocket and thrust it up his nostrils, gasping.

Mungo turned to me, coughing in the sickly haze. 'Would it be invisible flies he's seeing, do you think?'

'Could be some sort of sexual phobia. It's the way he keeps spraying her lap strikes me as ominous.'

The Haji, twitching his head at invisible attackers like a sleeping dog in the grip of a nightmare, fired salvoes of Carfresh in every direction. The Chinese lady in the front seat huddled into a corner staring fixedly ahead, her face stony, her trousers lacquered with congealed aerosol. A blue kilometre-post flashed by.

'Only a hundred and eighteen kilometres to go,' said Mungo.

I closed my eyes and tried to think of soothing music.

But on the trip from the orientation course, my first experience of the share-taxi system, the driver was at least as sane as the rest of us, and six hours later we were weaving our way down the High Street of that small Trengganu town, dodging goats, chickens and a vehicle called a trishaw which resembled a bathchair tied to a bicycle. It was raining, windy and muggy, like a Hebridean summer. On a building like a prison block was a sign which said HOTEL KASANYA. We had arrived.

Love in Pahang

In the event, Fiona found herself a house fairly quickly. Kuantan was building itself a new port several miles north of the town, and in anticipation of an economic boom an enormous number of new *tamans*, or suburban housing developments, had been built. Since then the structure of the quays had apparently subsided several feet into the mud, so they were having to start again. The opening of the port had duly been postponed, and landlords were begging potential tenants to take on houses at cut-price rents.

As a result of all this new building Kuantan now straggled widely in all directions, but it still remained one of the pleasantest towns in Malaysia, with a beautiful beach backed by forested hills as well as shopping facilities which after scruffy little Kuala Penyu seemed almost up to the Orchard Road level. If you arrived at one particular supermarket at the right time of day you could even buy wholemeal bread, a very un-Asian delicacy I used to develop a craving for.

Fiona's little end-of-terrace house was a great deal smaller than Mungo's palace, but being single-storey it had one particularly desirable feature in comparison, which was a functioning water supply. Mungo's huge detached house in Kuantan Garden, the town's classiest suburb, had innumerable bathrooms, like a film-set for some extravaganza about the last days of the Roman Empire, but the effect of sybaritic luxury was marred by the fact that only the downstairs taps worked. Apparently the water pressure was too low. I found myself thinking that few things make you feel more of an idiot than trudging upstairs in the house of someone you do not know very well carrying a large bucketful of water in order to flush one of three elegant upstairs lavatories, none of which are capable of doing the job by themselves.

About a month after moving into my own house I went to stay for the weekend with Mungo at the same time as Cyril, whom I had not seen since the end of the orientation course. I had already seen both Fiona and Mungo in Kuantan. Mungo was sunk in a depression. In addition to a fiery temper Fiona had both grace and vitality in abundance, and Mungo had obviously got used to having her to brighten his spartan palace for a week or two. Now it was a wrench for him to find himself coping with life on his own again. Like many men he had seen marriage as a very good reason for never bothering to acquire any domestic skills, and suddenly it was like having to conduct all his daily business in a language he spoke about five words of.

I sat in his kitchen drinking coffee, watching Fiona at work. It was a slow process of rehabilitation.

'Now listen, Mungo, because I'm not going to explain again. For a boiled egg, you put the thing in a pan of boiling water. For a fried egg you use a bit of oil and break your egg into it . . . like this. Now you take this wee spatula here . . . are you following me?'

'Aye, I can practise that later, it's only the washing machine I'm having problems with. If you could chust run through the instructions again for me afterwards . . .'

Weekends are a fairly straightforward business in most countries. In Malaysia there is a basic structural problem, because only the more Westernised states, or at least the ones with the largest non-Malay population, follow the familiar Saturday-Sunday weekend. The others follow a Muslim weekend in order to leave the holy day of Friday free. This means that they take Friday and Saturday off (and often Thursday afternoon too, since this is regarded as *malam Juma'at*, the eve of Friday), then go back to work on Sunday.

In an abstract sense, unless like the Lord's Day Observance Society you have strong feelings about Sunday as distinct from any other day of the week, this makes very little difference to life. Things are the same, but moved one day along, unlike in the Sultanate of Brunei which complicates the issue further by following a split weekend: Friday off, Saturday on, Sunday off. It does make for complications, though, when your own state (Trengganu) follows the 'Muslim' weekend while the neighbouring one (Pahang, which includes Kuantan) follows the other. Cyril was teaching three hours' drive south of Kuantan in the state of Johore, which also follows the Muslim weekend. This meant that the two of us were able to arrive at Mungo's house from opposite directions on Thursday evening, even though both he and Fiona would be at work the following morning.

I had sensed the way Cyril's feelings about Fiona were heading (I knew all about my own), and as I lay down to sleep under the spinning ceiling fan I wondered why it was that something so supposedly straightforward as sexual preference should end up getting elaborated into a kind of soap opera.

I was given plenty of opportunity to brood over it that night. Economic life in Malaysia being what it is, the majority of houses in up-market Kuantan Garden were inhabited by Chinese families. There was also an Indian who was a top gynaecologist, but as far as I knew there were no Malays. This meant that Kuantan Garden was free from the curse (I make no apology for speaking as an unbeliever) of a mosque with its overamplified muezzin blaring the call to the faithful through loudspeakers at five o'clock in the morning. There might have been a muezzin audible in the far distance, from some other part of town, but a distant muezzin is no hardship. It can even be an evocative sound, something you drowse through, barely conscious of any disturbance, a pleasant reminder that you are in a part of the world where the customs and the climate and the wildlife and the landscape are not like home.

On the other hand, though a local Malay majority subjects you to the sound of an old man groaning tunelessly into a load of disco equipment when you are trying to sleep, it protects you (thanks to Muslim *tabus*) from another kind of unwanted noise which I always found even more disturbing. Even the most long-winded *bilal*, or caller, will eventually be overtaken by a fit of coughing and switch off his microphone, or wander away for breakfast. In any case, however fanatical he may be, there are only five times a day appointed for Islamic prayer. Dogs, on the other hand, can start at any time, taking their cue from other dogs, from a cat sauntering past, from an early-morning jogger, from the moon, from the tail-end of a nightmare, from the configuration of the stars, from the sound of a ripe mango falling from a tree. And there is nothing to stop them after three or four minutes. Dogs, as the language reminds us, are nothing if not dogged.

Dogs, in fact, are the curse of affluent Malaysian suburbs, because every Chinese family expects to keep two or three of them. They do not keep them for company. They do not keep them because they find the ways of dogs interesting, still less so that Mr Breadwinner Tan will have something to welcome him home after a hard day at the office. Nor do they keep them to have company as they walk through the woods or along the beach. Nobody in tropical Asia goes for walks. They keep dogs in case of intruders, as an alarm system and a deterrent.

The dogs, in other words, are expected to bark, and this is exactly what they do. All day. All night. The sound stirs in the heavy silence of the tropical night as you lie half-awake, conscious only of the chirr-chirr-chirr of what might be either a bird or an insect or a tree-frog. A gecko calls – ch'k-ch'k-ch'k – from the landing. Along the distant main road, behind dense trees, a car passes. All these are sounds faint enough to be more or less drowned by the whirring of the fan or the hum of your neighbour's air-conditioner.

Then in the distance you hear a faint bark, repeated several times. It is not left alone for long. It is joined by another, and another, and then another: still very distant, still dream-compatible, a dim moon-barking on the horizon of your mind. But then there is a contagion, like coughing at classical concerts, or yawning at work. Soon the barking is a wave of sound, like the waves of sound on a recording of the humpback whale, or the waves of cicada-sound which rise and fall and overlap and cut into each other in the orchestra the rain-forest conducts at nightfall. Now you turn over peevishly in bed, trying to remember the password into a dissolving reverie. Alone on the endless prairies of insomnia you hear the wolves howling. There are big dogs that bay and little dogs that yap, and they have joined forces across the drowsing town.

Canine hysteria. The prisoners are rioting, every one of them chained to a chain-link fence inside a double-padlocked gate beside a parked Toyota, or Volvo, or Mercedes. At least the muezzin, you think with the pillow over your head and wads of Kleenex tissue in your ears, has claims to be an ancient and noble call to prayer. Like church bells . . . change-ringers . . . Treble Bob Major . . . oranges and lemons . . . but this is no call to anything except sullen resentment, nothing but a mindless frenzy, every yap and yelp a single separate particle of subhuman hysteria which is so pitched as to arouse some atavistic urge to respond: a well-aimed kick, a hurled boot, a shotgun.

Except that you are dealing not with a single marauding dog dogging the footsteps of your dreams but with a pack of them, a horde of them, a hideous choir of them: a disturbance of dogs, a deluge of dogs, a delirium of dogs, a delinquency of dogs, a deformity of dogs, a damnation of dogs, a dimwittedness of dogs, a dunghill of dogs doggerwauling through the night, diminuendo and crescendo and somehow diminuendo again, because it is daylight and you are rising to the surface of sleep for a second time, dog-tired, with only a dog or two left doggedly saluting the dawn.

And in the meantime every house in Kuantan Garden could have been broken into, burgled, burnt to the ground, and what alarm could possibly have been raised? Every night the dogs cry wolf. And every Chinese family sleeps through the malfunctioning of its organic alarm system like a baby in a cradle in the corner of the living-room which sleeps, milky and unconcerned, through the gunfire on the TV every night.

Cyril and I faced each other warily across the breakfast table. Mungo had already left for school. We addressed one another with scrupulous politeness.

'Good morning, Peter. I trust you slept well.'

'Fine, fine. Bit of dog trouble, I suppose. How about you?'

'Oh, not too bad. You're right about the dogs. Bit too much of a good thing, I thought.'

'Absolutely. Noisy creatures, dogs.'

'Rather a nuisance, in fact, when you're trying to sleep.'

'I quite agree. Can I make you some toast?'

'Well, that's very good of you. I'll look after the drinks. Tea or coffee?'

'Whatever you're having, thanks, Cyril.'

We prattled on in this brittle Wodehousian fashion as we ate. The conversation, rudderless, drifted towards teaching.

'Of course,' said Cyril, 'we're not completely tied to grammar-based teaching on this course. There are all sorts of other ways of using language in class. Discussions, for example.'

'Oh yes, quite. Except that it can sometimes seem a bit artificial, don't you think, setting up a profound serious discussion in the classroom. You know, nuclear power or feminism or something, just as though it had happened spontaneously and the class didn't know damn' well it was just one more English lesson and the teacher weren't bored stiff with everyone's opinions. Including his own.'

By now Cyril had finished his toast and marmalade. He pushed his plate away. The preliminaries were over, and it was time for the serious discussions to start. He began to speak in capitals.

'As we're having a profound and serious discussion ourselves, Peter, may I Touch on a Topic Close to my Heart?'

I had been neatly trapped into giving him his cue. My heart sank. 'Beer?' I said, trying to deflect what I knew was coming.

But Cyril, given new vitality by the wholemeal bread of Kuantan, was not to be put off by flippancy. The capital letters grew more frequent. It was like something out of a Regency novel.

'Am I to understand that You and I are Rivals for the Affections of the Fair Fiona?'

There was an awkward silence. I had been brought up with a prejudice against kissing-and-telling, and there were various things I was not free to say. I said at last, rather feebly, 'Well, you'd better ask Fiona, hadn't you?'

It was meant to close the discussion. Cyril would have been more constructively occupied making more coffee, or cleaning his teeth. He chose to bulldoze his way on. It was like a military operation. There was no deflecting him.

'Come on, now.' He wagged a finger.

I did my best to shrug the whole thing off. 'Well,' I said vaguely. 'I'm . . . interested in Fiona.'

'A-*ha*,' said Cyril, and went upstairs to clean his teeth. I made some more coffee for myself and thought unflattering thoughts about romantic love.

We were due to meet Fiona at a café in town around lunch-time. It was Friday, the day of the *sembahyang Juma'at*, the big Friday prayers, and lessons at Kuantan Science School finished an hour early in order to give the Malay pupils time to prepare for this. The minutes dragged by, and no Fiona came. The ice in my second glass of lemon tea began to melt.

In fact (as it turned out later) she had been held up at school because Stuart Robertson had been even more than his usual insufferable self that morning, leaving her with a string of administrative problems to sort out. In the meantime the gaps of silence in our conversation at Saté Raya grew longer.

'I wonder,' said Cyril musingly after the longest gap of all, 'if three mightn't be . . . one too many.'

'It always is. We'll just have to juggle it tactfully, won't we?'

The bulldozer drove inexorably on. 'But Fiona definitely said she wanted to see us both separately.'

I was ready for him to say 'Pistols at dawn' at any moment, but before he had the chance to make any further comment Fiona appeared with Mungo, full of apologies for herself and fulminations against Stuart Robertson. Looking back, I have a great deal of sympathy for her; she was starting a new job in a new country while coping with one lunatic colleague, one male would-be divorcé weeping on her shoulder, another hungry for the chance to make his romantic intentions clear with a bouquet of orchids, and myself. In the circumstances she was coping rather well.

She had already bought a second-hand car. It was small, bright yellow and not wholly reliable. Late that afternoon she, Cyril and I drove down a bumpy track to a lonely stretch of the northbound highway to have a look at the sea before the sun went down. As we climbed the steep hill which led to the highway the engine began to misfire. Eventually, about five miles out of town, the noises turned ominous. Fiona pulled on the verge of the highway at a point where it crossed a declivity in the forest. The car sounded as though it were about to explode at any minute.

We thumbed down a small passing van with an Indian and a Malay in it and struggled to pool what little we had gleaned from the periods of language instruction which had been scattered rather half-heartedly through the orientation course.

'Our car . . . *kereta* . . . what's "broken down"?'

'*Rosak.*' It was one of the most useful words in the language.

'Oh yes. *Kereta rosak.*' We stabbed our fingers in the direction of the town. Every trace of habitation was hidden by the huge trees which lined the forest's edge on both sides. We might have been half-way along the Trans-Amazon Highway. There was not much daylight left.

The Indian nodded. '*Satu orang.* One person.'

With admirable decisiveness Fiona got into the van, which roared off promptly.

'Really,' said Cyril, 'she shouldn't have . . . I mean, *anything* . . .' His voice trailed away.

'I know. I'm kicking myself because I never even got the number.'

'What about the trade name?'

'I didn't get that either.'

'Dear me. Nor did I.'

'Well, it's too late to worry now. And if you were thinking you ought to have gone instead of her, Cyril, I feel just the same about myself. But she's a pretty decisive person. I don't honestly think we could have stopped her.'

'Decisive . . . yes, I suppose she is. Quite a strong personality, wouldn't you say?'

'Strong enough to look after herself, I should think.' I was not entirely convinced by my words.

Cyril stared back for a moment along the highway, where the anonymous van had long since disappeared in the direction of Kuantan. I had the impression that he had never come across a girl like Fiona before. But then, neither had I.

We looked out at the forest trees beneath the slope of the ridge we were on, like a railway viaduct. There was impending rain in the sky. I felt a twinge of worry about Fiona, but at the same time a strong sense of the utterly ridiculous nature of the situation. A sudden picture came into my mind of one of us volunteering, like an equatorial version of Captain Oates on Scott's expedition, to walk out into the forest and never return.

I had the remains of a packet of small cigars with me, and we shared the last two in a spirit of slightly strained companionship as we strolled along the verge. We made desultory conversation, blowing clouds of smoke as a prophylactic against mosquitoes and kicking invading ants from our feet.

'There don't seem to be as many birds about as you'd expect,' said Cyril.

'Perhaps they're roosting.'

'Oh, there goes one. Or perhaps it was a bat.'

'There's one. No, it was a huge butterfly.'

'Look how much darker it's got in the last five minutes or so.'

And so it had. At that moment the forest noises began. We could hear the continuous stridencies of cicadas and the sharp calls of monkeys. The huge trees were silhouetted against the evening sky. Suddenly the forest to either side of us was a living thing, and the world was infinite. It was as though a storm had suddenly risen above a placid sea. I listened to it all, rapt, with the whole ridiculous rivalry forgotten.

But the rain started before we had time to appreciate things fully, and we took shelter in the car. Fiona was back within the hour with a helpful primary school headmaster she knew and a mechanic. By the time we had devoured a banana-leaf curry at a Hindu Indian restaurant in town the electrical short which had caused the breakdown was mended. The repair bill came to the equivalent of three pounds.

Later in the evening we went on to meet Mungo at a bar-restaurant run by an engaging Chinese called Benny Kim. Benny was a friend of Mungo's. He was said to be an ex-gangster who had found Singapore too hot for him. He was a sleek affable man in his mid-thirties with slicked-back hair and something calculating in his expression.

Like most Chinese, Benny Kim was a keen gambler. The lottery system in Malaysia is known as the *empat nombor*, which means four-digit. There is an insatiable demand for supposedly lucky four-figure numbers to feed into it. The Chinese attitude to numbers is obsessive, a blend of system and superstition. New car licence numbers, permutations of birth-dates: anything will do. Benny had somehow found out that the number of Fiona's newish *taman* house ran to four figures.

It was not clear why it needed to be numbered in the thousands when two figures would have served the purpose. But at any rate it was a four-figure number, and there was a personal connection about it, and that was enough for Benny.

'You must give me the number of your house, Fiona. Could be lucky.'

Fiona, understandably, was wary. There are other

reasons why a man might want to find out the address of a girl living alone. 'I just want your number so I can buy it in the lottery' sounds unconvincing to Western ears. She kept smiling, always a sensible thing to do in South-East Asia, and stalled.

'Oh, but Benny, the post don't deliver because there isn't a letter-box yet, and I haven't learned the number.'

'But the number is written on the house-lah.'

'Well, Benny, I'm afraid I haven't really looked. I'm not good about numbers, honestly.'

He smiled and probed; she smiled and parried. In the end he gave up and told us a story about a European girl who had been staying a little way up the coast from Kuantan. As he talked, I recognised the familiar Eastern complaint about the inscrutability of Westerners.

'So this, you see, very attractive girl, when I meet her one day, I ask her out. We have a meal, I buy her a present, cost a lo' of money, but she don't want. She say to me, okay, Benny, we just friends, no more-lah.

'So I think okay, maybe she already got some rich friend, I forget abou' her. Then later I see her again. She is with this Malay boy, this very young Malay, got long hair, ve-ree brown skin, ve-ree poor. And she is spending so much time with him all the rest of the time she is on holiday here. And I think *Wha-at?*'

Benny spread his hands wide. 'Listen, this I don' never understand. Okay, if I am poor, I understand maybe she don' like me. But I am not poor. I got plenty, buy her ring, clothings, anything she want-lah. So why she go with this boy, this Malay, got no money, good in swimming, playing guitar only? He don' buy her ring, don' buy her clothings, can't buy nothing 'cause so poor-lah. So why she don' like me better?'

He pushed another bottle of beer towards Mungo. 'European girls . . . I ne-ver understand why they do like this.'

I thought of brown lithe Malay bodies, the easy companionship, a month's idyll of sea-water and sand and tropical heat and simplicity an ocean away from workaday life in

Frankfurt or Stockholm, and understood very clearly. But there was no way I could explain to Benny Kim. The Chinese, in my experience, are the most cold-bloodedly realistic people in the world. To them anything done for gain or family advancement justifies itself in a way very few other things in life do, so that they readily come to see Westerners as frivolous, adolescent, self-indulgent.

At the same time they have an intensely Puritanical streak. If Benny had come to understand the motives of a European girl who had chosen sex-plus-romance with a beautiful penniless Malay boy, he would have been disgusted as well as scornful.

MONSOON NIGHT

The rain casts nets of water
Round the house; its walls
Softly close off the world.

What can the fan do
To stir thoughts that are held
Trapped by this endless rain?

Thoughts themselves are a cage
Within that other, liquid
Cage of woven rain.

The latticed fern, the cane
Bookshelves weave enclosures:
Fern and furniture.

I sit alone within nets,
Walls, cages of rain.
You are ninety miles away:

I cannot believe in roads,
Am only free to tell
Myself how the rain dissolves

Its moving chains of glass,
Its transparent lattices,
Each moment of the night.

A Meal in Rat Alley

Eventually the deluges of the extended monsoon began to lessen. School life slowly lost something of its bizarre aspect, as everything does sooner or later. Some chemical response inside you, in sheer self-defence, causes a coating of familiarity to form on the oddness of things, and before you know what has happened you are beginning to kick against the routine all over again, craving something new.

In the equatorial forest belt there are countries – not so much Malaysia, more obviously the Philippines, parts of West Africa and tropical America – where slash-and-burn cultivators are a problem. They move in to a stretch of forest where the loggers have selectively felled the most desirable timber trees, systematically tame and clear it with fire and axe, then find that the soil underneath is only good enough for a couple of harvests. There is not much long-term fertility in the soil of most of these equatorial regions once the trees have been cleared; the cycle of decay is too rapid in that overwhelmingly hot and humid climate, so that the roots of the trees are already sucking nourishment from their own fallen leaves before these have had a chance to form much in the way of topsoil. Dig around the roots and in a few inches you will find yourself down to the sticky orange clay which underlies the thin soil.

The rainfall – ninety, a hundred and fifty, two hundred inches a year depending which coast you are on, how far inland, how high up, which side of the nearest mountain range – completes the job once the trees are cleared. The minerals and nutrients are leached, meaning not sucked by jungle-dwelling worms but driven deep down into the inaccessible clay subsoil as though by a high-pressure hose. On the gullied and compacted surface the choking, inedible, impassable, all-but-indestructible *lalang* grass takes over.

And at this point the slash-and-burn cultivator, finding his crops stunted or choked, moves on to start the process all over again. *Tomorrow to fresh Woods and Pastures new*; but here there is nothing of the Arcadian temperate idyll about it. The fresh woods are for the axe, and the *lalang* grass which looks from a distance like pasture on the hillside is a waist-high waste-land good for neither man nor beast. The whole business struck me as an apt metaphor for what restless people do with their lives.

But I had not reached this stage yet. I was satisfied at having survived my first term and turned that gloomy barn of a house into something which felt more or less like home. I had seen more of Kuantan, but there were to be no shared holiday plans with Fiona. The rivalry with Cyril was already beginning to seem like a newsmagazine account of an electoral campaign overtaken by the election itself: interesting to a historian, perhaps, but no longer current affairs. Cyril and I, if you like, had seen our rivalry as a kind of election campaign between two candidates. But in the long term, neither of us was chosen. Fiona had been swayed by a third candidate neither Cyril nor I had seen as a threat: her own independent unattached life. In the meantime some trees had been cleared, but the soil underneath had not been good for much of a harvest.

Which is why I had been sitting on that wave-washed rocky outcrop above Robinson Crusoe Bay, mildly pink with the sun on the outside, decidedly blue on the inside, like some sort of half-cooked lobster, brooding over the way life, if you give it its head and stop trying to twist it in your own direction, always ambles on in the direction of anti-climax. Which (in turn) is why the whole episode, in the long run, had to turn into a comedy.

You get stiff, trying to hold any other kind of pose for long. I slid down from my solitary eminence, lacerating my backside in the process, and trudged back into the world of mundane comedy.

On the final evening of term the teachers and ancillary staff went back to the school for a *jamuan*, a celebratory meal in the main hall. For a Westerner it was an odd mixture of formality and informality, relaxed but with no trace of spontaneity or high spirits. It was what Malays understand by a party.

I sometimes used to try to imagine what Malay life would have been like if Islam, with its prohibition against alcohol, had never reached the Straits of Malacca. Certainly those ethnic and linguistic cousins of the Malays the Ibans of Sarawak (the tribe once called Sea Dayaks) drink abundantly and are a far more outgoing people. 'They are more lively,' wrote Alfred Russel Wallace something over a hundred years ago, 'more talkative, less secretive, and less suspicious than the Malay, and therefore pleasanter companions.' There is something in Malay life which refuses to admit either nervous tension or the high spirits which are the natural reaction against it. The prevailing tone of things is gentle, even-tempered, unaggressive, smiling but without much obvious amusement. 'In character' (to quote Wallace again)

> the Malay is impassive. He exhibits a reserve, diffidence and even bashfulness, which is in some degree attractive. He is not demonstrative. His feelings of surprise, admiration or fear, are never openly manifested, and are probably not strongly felt. When alone the Malay is taciturn; he neither talks nor sings to himself. He is cautious of giving offence to his equals. Practical joking is utterly repugnant to his disposition; for he is particularly sensitive to breaches of etiquette, or any interference with the personal liberty of himself or another.

There was certainly no alcohol at this particular *jamuan*, or at any other. I am not a heavy drinker myself, but I realised after some months in Malaysia that there is all the difference in the world between even a light drinker from an alcohol-culture and someone from a culture where alcohol is *tabu*. Among Muslims it is not that you miss the spectacle of people picking fights with everyone around them or collapsing in a drunken stupor under the table. It is simply that you feel the absence of something which helps to make life easier and also to bring out the quality of human warmth in it, a sort of anti-freeze-plus-lubricating-oil for the social machine. At the end-of-term 'party' at the Science School there were only jugs of a sickly crimson liquid tasting of synthetic rose essence. This did not help the speeches to pass any easier.

Malays have a great tolerance of speechmaking. The Malay 'is slow and deliberate in speech' (Wallace again), 'and circuitous in introducing the subject he has come expressly to discuss.' The duration is pretty carefully calculated according to rank; the higher this is, the longer the speech you are entitled to make.

The gathering – there were about seventy of us – assembled along a square arch-formation of tables, one beneath the stage and the others along both sides of the hall. The Malays segregated themselves carefully according to sex; the non-Muslims mingled more casually. We were about to sit down and start eating after a few introductory words from the Chairman of the Staff Welfare Committee when a droning persistent chant made itself heard through the clattering of chairs and tentative buzz of conversation. It was the *ustaz*, the religious teacher.

The name of the *ustaz* was Musa, which is the Muslim equivalent of Moses. He was a thickset man bearing some resemblance to a reduced-scale version of the Rev. Ian Paisley, if Mr Paisley can be imagined wearing what looked from a distance like a Jewish skull-cap. The *ustaz* Musa, with an expression of stern other-worldliness on his generally inexpressive face, had launched into a series of prayers. We waited until he had chanted himself to a standstill.

He took no visible interest in the rest of the proceedings, with the exception of the food. His expression during the other speeches, which came at the end of the meal, suggested that he regarded them as beneath his notice.

The last, and longest, speech was given by Encik

Shamsuddin Mohidin the headmaster, someone I found pleasant enough to deal with but so remote in manner as to be unknowable. He was a tall rather gangling man who could be seen early most mornings stalking delicately around the open landings which ran along the side of every classroom, checking (I suppose) that none of his staff had neglected their lessons and gone straight to the canteen for breakfast. His voice was so gentle as to be almost as inaudible as Stuart Robertson's.

His speech was enlivened by the antics of the handsome grey-and-white cat from the canteen, which strolled in as elegantly as an Edwardian dandy in morning suit and white spats and sat by his table looking up at him as he spoke with its Asian bat-ears pricked. On its face was an expression of more intelligence and animation than I had seen the *ustaz* Musa manage. Towards the end of the speech it yawned prominently. I could have sworn it raised one paw and glanced at a watch hidden among the fur. It then leapt on to the table and started to attack a dish of chicken curry. At this point it was forcibly, though not roughly, removed.

This was the point when a drink to nurse would have been welcome. There was no such thing to be had, and perhaps as a result there was nothing to make people linger at the end. Something I never got used to was the way Asian meals – Chinese as well as Malay, Singaporean as well as Malaysian – stopped quite suddenly, as though some sort of dog-whistle I could not hear had been blown. With the Chinese the final mouthful of food was the cue for departure, with the Malays the closing formulae of the final speech. Nobody except Westerners (those inscrutable Westerners again) lingers. The Headmaster's speech trickled to its conclusion, chairs shuffled, and already people were starting to leave the table.

The whole ceremony (it was not really a party at all) had lasted exactly one hour. Nobody wished each other a good holiday, or said anything on the lines of 'See you in two weeks' time.' Softly and silently, like the victims of Lewis Carroll's Boojum, they melted away. Not with a bang, scarcely even with a whimper, the term had ended.

It was not long after this that a new, even larger batch of teachers from Britain and Australia arrived on the same project. They in turn had to pass through the initiation rites at the Federal Hotel in Kuala Lumpur, and I was one of various teachers who were hauled in from our schools to give help with the course.

I left Jim grumbling. The Trengganu State Education Department had ordered the launching of a drama competition for Form One pupils in the state. If I had stayed, we could have worked on the Science School's contribution together. Now he was left to manage the whole business by himself. Desmond, an altogether less affable and more forbidding person, had not been approached by the Headmaster. Jim was paying the penalty for being approachable, not to mention scrupulously careful about his personal hygiene.

The play was later put on in the school hall in the presence of judges for the competition. No pupils were admitted to watch. The dictates of the State Education Department had to be obeyed, but that did not prevent drama, when performed in public, from being unacceptable to informed Muslim opinion. It had something to do with the fact that it involved boys watching girls, even appearing on the same stage as them. The complementary fact that the children involved were only thirteen made no difference. Local opinion, guided by *Ustaz* Musa and his even more formidable female counterpart *Ustazah* Siti Fatimah, would have seen only a difference of degree, not one of essence, between *One-Act Plays for Malaysian Schools* and *Oh, Calcutta*.

Back at the Federal Hotel things were not peaceful. There was a frantic construction boom going on in Kuala Lumpur at the time. A couple of years later it would show its effects in the form of the lowest hotel occupancy rates in East Asia. At the time everyone with a few million dollars to invest (which seemed to mean a surprisingly large number of people in Malaysia) was getting in on the act, and an eighteen-storey hotel was going up in a cramped enclosure behind the swimming-pool of the Federal. Lectures and workshop sessions would be regularly punctuated by the sound of a piledriver: 'Now at this KER-THOONK I'm going to split you up into KER-THOONK and ask each group to KER-THOONK a lesson plan to incorporate some of these KER-THOONK so would someone like to KER-THOONK these handouts?' It was all a bit of a shock after the coconut palms and kampong lanes of the Trengganu coast.

The second evening I was there some sort of underground pipe was ruptured when the land behind the swimming-pool subsided. Either the building contractors had miscalculated, or the man operating the JCB had fallen asleep on the job. As a result both the hot water and the air-conditioning failed. The following evening the air-conditioning went off again, accompanied this time by the cold water. You found yourself staggering back to your room along unventilated corridors with the temperature in the thirties Celsius, images of cool glittering water dancing in front of you. At the shower or the wash-basin you would then find nothing but clouds of steam and scalding torrents, as in some ingenious punishment from the Underworld of Greek mythology. Nerves were soon frayed.

In some interlude between scribbling notes of questions asked at various lectures I went downstairs for a swim, mirages dancing in front of me. An uncompromising notice by the poolside, quivering in the heat, said DANGER: POOL CLOSED.

After a brief respite the cold water went off again the following day, with nothing but a trickle of mud oozing from the tap, but at least by now the notice beside the swimming-pool had been taken down. Unforunately everyone else was haunted by the same enticing mirages of cool translucent water, so that when I took my towel down to the pool I found it crammed from end to end, uninvitingly, with pink bad-tempered hotel guests. The entire Danish badminton team, after a stand-up row with the hotel manager, had checked out a couple of hours before in search of somewhere cooler. They had my sympathy. Badminton, a game taken extremely seriously in Malaysia, is played indoors. Neither fans nor air-conditioning are allowed in order to keep the air absolutely still. Huge crowds turn up at the National Stadium to watch, and the result is a pretty steamy atmosphere. It seemed reasonable of the players to expect a bit of cool during the daytime, at least. Perhaps the Danes were already looking back with some nostalgia to the Scandinavian winter they had just survived.

On the Muzak system, which unfortunately was unaffected by any of the disturbance, a piano and orchestra played a lobotomised version of the 'Ode to Joy' from Beethoven's Ninth Symphony, without conviction. The glamour of 'international-class' hotels was beginning to wear a bit thin.

The air-conditioning was eventually restored, and a straggle of guests mopping their brows in the hotel lobby cheered feebly. I retreated to the coffee-shop and began to sneeze. Perversely, I had caught a cold.

I drank hot lemon tea, feeling sorry for myself. The void in my private life was bad enough; to be struck down by snivelling catarrh seemed like personal malice on the part of those in high places. It was late in the evening, and business at the coffee-shop was quiet. I stared out at the traffic and irrelevant glitter of Jalan Bukit Bintang and brooded. I was thirty-eight, and it seemed to me that my youth was more or less used up. It was a depressing thought.

It was one of those moments when the appeal of travel, of being far from home (like that of the 'international-class' luxury of the malfunctioning hotel I was being paid to stay at) begins to seem a bit fraudulent. I had sometimes thought of myself, admittedly in a joking kind of way, as a solitary explorer, but what had happened to that solitary explorer Gauld now? His condition was critical, and by all accounts the prognosis was not hopeful. Who else was going to carry my name on into middle-age? Gauld the philosopher, pipe-smoking, tweedy and balding? Gauld the melancholy dissipated alcoholic, mumbling into his glass 'It would all be different if they'd published my novel' . . . ? Gauld the cynical middle-aged careerist with hard lines around his mouth?

Hardly the latter, when the thought of any kind of further academic study made me cringe. I had met another English teacher working for the same company who was doing his MA in Applied Linguistics ('absolutely essential if you want to get on'). The dissertation he had to write as part of this was fifty thousand words long, which is the length of a short novel. The subject was 'Interruptions' Except as a conversation-stopper, I could not see a lot to be gained from this. Nor could I believe in any of those middle-aged selves I was creating for myself.

What was thirty-eight, anyway? Not young exactly, but then on the other hand the phrase 'middle-aged' had become devalued in English; it seemed to mean 'approaching retirement age', which in my case felt a depressingly long way off. What was I? In my prime, I supposed. I had never felt less like it. I sucked at a slice of lemon on the off-chance that the vitamin C might do my cold good and reached for a Kleenex tissue.

I was trapped in a particular mood, unable to enjoy staying up and yet unwilling to face going to bed. I ordered more tea, and the young Chinese waiter stopped for a chat. His name was Dan. He was garrulous and friendly.

'Mister Peter, you write to me when you leave, okay?'

From the blurring cloud of my incipient cold and unattached-man's depression I looked back at him, trying to read the signs. Was Dan just an innocent who found me approachable, or did he think I was a homosexual looking for a pick-up? Both would have fitted the evidence.

One of the new Australian teachers quite obviously was a homosexual cruising in search of pick-ups. I had seen him passing the door of the hotel several times, each time with a different handsome boy in tow. With a very different ache in my heart I considered this. From some kind of planetary point of view, I supposed – as if you were observing human behaviour from the standpoint of a different, Martian, metabolism – it would simply seem like a variation on the same basic theme, minor key instead of major. From a human point of view (at least from my own, for what that was worth) it just seemed . . . I groped for the right word: not perverted necessarily, but – since there was an opposite sex after all – perverse.

'I fetch you more tea, Mr Peter?' It was Dan, surprisingly bright-eyed and effusive considering it was not far short of midnight.

I shook my head and got up to go. 'No thanks, Dan,' I said. 'I think I've had just about enough.'

Behind the traffic-choked thoroughfare of Jalan Bukit Bintang was a narrow street called Jalan Alor, otherwise known as Rat Alley, which came to life in the evening as an open-air food-market in the form of an avenue of crowded Chinese restaurants and hawker stalls. Sitting with a group of us at a circular table on the pavement one evening, a small pugnacious teacher from South Wales held forth on his first unflattering impressions of South-East Asia. He had been teaching on the Spanish Mediterranean, and this was his first time outside Europe. I think he had expected to find something like a winterless version of Spain – all countries with warm climates being the same sort of thing, after all, from a certain point of view – and was disconcerted by the foreignness of it all. A few things in Malaysia are surprisingly 'British', but nothing very much is 'European' in the sense of resembling France or Spain or Germany or Italy.

'Christ, things seem bloody expensive yer.'

It seemed an unlikely complaint, unless you expected to live only on gift-wrapped laver-bread and cockles air-freighted from the Gower Peninsula. I rose to the defence of Malaysia.

'What about public transport? The coaches are as cheap as anywhere in the world. Seventeen dollars from where I live down to Johore Bahru, just a bus-ride away from Singapore. That's five pounds for three hundred and fifty miles.'

He sneered. 'You're out of touch, boyo. We got new rates on the coaches at home now, see. There's been a shake-up. Swansea-London is next to nothing now.'

'Well then, what about taxis here in KL? They cost about a tenth of what they do in London.'

The Welshman's lip curled. 'I dunno about bloody London, man. I'm talking about Swansea.'

It was hard to summon up much enthusiasm for this conversation. I gestured at the laden table our group was sitting round. 'All right, I grant you the beer's expensive, but what about the food? Look at all this. You can eat like a king here, and you'll still find it hard to get the bill much above ten dollars a head.'

'Bloody coolie food. Back in Swansea you can get proper food, boyo. Meat and potatoes and two veg. Don't expect to pay much for bloody *rice*.'

He waved a hand dismissively at dishes heaped with chili prawns, sizzling beef with ginger and spring onion, a sweet-and-sour fish a foot long and five kinds of vegetables. 'Bloody coolie food,' he said for the second time. 'Can't get anything like a decent meat pie yer. Got bloody wonderful meat pies in Swansea. There's real food for you, boyo. And cheap, too.'

I had to remind myself that 'culture shock' makes people behave in odd ways. What seems at the time to be rudeness

or stupidity may simply be the result of a kind of panic, people trying desperately to call up a helpful image of Home (or the last country they worked in, which may come to the same thing) as they feel themselves drowning in unfamiliarity. There was an equally aggressive young Australian in the same group whose experience of Asia was limited to a week's holiday among the surfmats and pizzerias of Kuta Beach, Bali.

'Listen,' he said after an admittedly interminable series of talks on adjusting to Asian attitudes, which might well have appeared patronising to someone who knew Asia well. 'It's all very well for you Poms to have to sit through all this crap. You don't know anything about Asia. Us Aussies, we live next door to the place. We don't need to be bloody told about how to behave here. I don't need to be told all this shit about non-confrontation. I know it already, see?'

'Yes, I can see you do.'

At the end of the orientation course he and his wife took advantage of an escape-clause in the contract and went back to Australia. Under the snarl and the verbal pugilistics he was frightened. Newcomers to a country, if they wish to survive, have to cultivate big ears and a small mouth. He could not do it. He was simply incapable of turning off his aggressiveness even for five minutes.

The most distinguished guest speaker on the course was the perceptive and delightful Malay journalist and writer Adibah Amin. Her talk was on 'Malay Culture', and while her manner remained gentle, she pulled no punches. 'Why do Malays have this thing about Islam these days?' someone asked from the audience. 'If what you're saying is true, why are they turning so intolerant?'

Adibah Amin's answer was concise and memorable. 'Because Malays feel weak,' she said, 'and religion makes them feel strong.'

'Bit of a feeble talk, that,' said one of the Australians to me afterwards. 'She didn't seem able to say anything directly.'

Australian candour and earthiness, like Australian generosity, can be very refreshing. In their intense dislike of ceremony and gentleness Australians are about as far removed from Malays as it is possible to be. But the unfortunate thing about being obsessively direct, even crude, is that you find it hard to get any insight into all those many cultures in the world which have an element of hierarchy, of subtlety, of finesse, of ceremony. 'Load of friggin' nonsense,' says the Australian when confronted with such devious dealers as the Japanese, the Javanese, the French, the English upper middle class. 'Not like me, mate. I'm direct. I'm natural. I say what I think. It's the other bastards that are full of shit.'

But as any non-Australian could point out, Aussie ways are just as hard for foreigners to get used to as any other in the world. For many newcomers to Australia the cult of the Stubbie and the shout must be as arcane as the Japanese tea ceremony, and an obsession with all-male team sport is no more 'natural' or unaffected than an obsession with unarmed combat or kite-flying or Anglo-Catholic rites or bullfighting. Australians believe that they have no ceremonies or mysteries, that they are a nation of ordinary blokes behaving with total unaffected naturalness. Their neighbours in East Asia sometimes see them differently. Chinese businessmen-refugees from Hong Kong have to make an effort to learn the complex rituals of talking about sport in Sydney, just as the businessman from Perth has to take lessons in the art of bowing before he goes to clinch the deal in Osaka.

The English, of course (in case anyone should think I am exalting them at the expense of everyone else), can be as bad. I once flew from London to Thessaloniki in Northern Greece. Half the other passengers on the plane were elderly people from Lancashire who had won a week's seaside holiday in Khalkidhiki in a competition. They were not cosmopolitan travellers. As the disembarking passengers divided into two queues on the way to Immigration, the Manchester couple in front of me stopped and looked up in puzzlement at the two large notices overhead which said (in English as well as Greek) ← GREEKS and → FOREIGNERS.

'Eeeh,' said the husband to his wife at last, shaking his head in what appeared to be genuine bewilderment, 'that's the first time Ah've ivver been called a foreigner before.'

This tone of tolerant, slightly patronising wisdom is easier in retrospect than it was at the time, when I would sometimes find myself seething at what seemed like the endless Western tendency to bloody-minded aggressiveness. Did some of these people have nothing in their lives to sweeten their tempers? Was their whole attitude to life based on picking a quarrel with it? Could they only manage to communicate with other people by engineering a confrontation with them? And why had some of them bothered to leave their own countries in the first place?

Some kinds of misunderstanding were more innocent. There was a Scottish girl who got out of the bus from the airport and looked up in some puzzlement at the typical Kuala Lumpur afternoon sky: blue, white and grey in roughly equal proportions, bright sunshine for the moment but with the clouds thickening and the possibility of a downpour before sunset.

'I didn't think the weather would be like this,' she said. 'I thought the sun always shone in the tropics.'

There had been a lot to put up with lately. I said with heavy irony: 'They have a thing in this part of the world called the rain-forest. Ever wonder why they call it that?'

Her brow wrinkled. 'Oh . . . I didn't think it rained much here.'

There were six new teachers to join Jim, Desmond and myself. They were all Australian. Including spouses and children that made fifteen people to be transported to Kuala Penyu. I left them gathering together a convoy of share-taxis and second-hand cars and took a flight to Kuala Trengganu: an hour or so in the air, looking down on the whorls and loops of contour-planted oil palms by the million, like gigantic thumbprints on the rolling land, then the floating clouds and wooded ridges of Taman Negara, the peninsular National Park.

I had forgotten how attractive the half-hour drive was from the little airport back into Kuala Trengganu. It passed through a cultivated stretch of lowland, more like 'countryside' to a European eye than much of Malaysia with its forest, scrub and tree-crop plantations. The picture which comes into my mind is from later in the year, after the rice-harvest, in November: a chequered pattern of yellow and green *padi* fields with stooks of harvested rice here and there so that it brought back memories of Suffolk in an August heat-wave.

There were tall *tembusu* trees, upright and leafy, along the edges of the fields like hedgerow elms, and the whole landscape was bathed in that warm golden late-afternoon light which in the tropics barely gives you time to catch your breath before it starts to fade.

The share-taxi down the coast road to Kuala Penyu was memorable in other ways. I was not in a position (literally) to appreciate the landscape as I was wedged into a corner of the back seat beside a Malay family consisting of father, mother and one small boy. A couple of chickens were squeezed between our feet chuckling thoughtfully to themselves. The durian season had begun (it was the end of May), and there was a pervasive smell of that extraordinary fruit in the air: sickly, faintly foetid and yet curiously intriguing. The boot of the taxi must have been full of them. For another couple of months that smell would haunt the whole of equatorial South-East Asia from southern Thailand to the Moluccas.

The small boy was fed with a rambutan early in the journey and proceeded to throw it up over his father twenty minutes later. His parents cleared up the mess with that unruffled Malay patience I never failed to admire, and when I moved my feet further away the chickens protested in a sleepy absent-minded sort of way. The muzak of the Federal Hotel seemed to belong to another civilisation, more fragile and at the same time less convincing. It was a true East Coast homecoming.

PART THREE

The Variegation of Existence

The fundamental Malaysian distinction within its own population is between Malay and non-Malay, and the newcomer who naively says 'I can't tell the difference between them' is not allowed to remain ignorant for long. Malays are *bumiputra*, which is normally translated as 'sons of the soil', but literally *putra* means 'princes' rather than 'sons'.

The implication of the word is that they alone are the real inhabitants. Everyone else is regarded as some kind of immigrant except the native tribes of Malaysian Borneo and the few remaining *orang asli* or aborigines who still eke out an existence in the forested central highlands of the peninsula. These various non-Malay native groups are accepted rather grudgingly as second-class *bumiputra* unless they are Muslims, in which case they are seen as useful election-fodder and encouraged to think of themselves as Malays.

I once found myself looking idly at the whiteboard in the headmaster's office while he spoke to the District Education Office on the telephone. On the board was a breakdown of the fifty or so staff according to ethnic group. The majority were listed as *Melayu* or Malay, eight were *Cina* or Chinese, one (Navamalar) was *India* and ten were *Lain-lain* which means Others. It was a curious distinction, since of these ten nine were either British or Australian, in other words obviously foreign, and the tenth, a gentle friendly man called Feen Edeng, was a Malaysian of Thai descent from Kelantan, near the border with Thailand. Apparently the fact that he was neither Malay, Chinese nor Indian was considered more important than the fact that he (unlike the nine of us Westerners) was a Malaysian citizen.

Even odder was the case of a girl called Faroushee, who came during my second year, Faroushee was Singapore-

Muslim by birth and had emigrated across the Causeway to Malaysia. She was Indian and Arab by descent ('not a drop of Malay blood in me,' she used to say with amusement and a trace of perverse pride) and fluent in both Malay and English. After two years in Malaysia she was now listed in the Malay column on the headmaster's whiteboard, eligible for the various goodies the Malaysian government reserves for those of its citizens it considers native: all sorts of subsidised higher education abroad, assured promotion over the heads of non-Malay colleagues, even the opportunity to invest her money in a special *Bumiputra*-only savings scheme (*Amanah Saham Nasional*) which would give her seventeen per cent interest while the rest of the country, the *lain-lain*, including Chinese and non-Muslim Indians, had to be content with the standard three per cent or so. Her religion, to the Malaysian authorities, was what really mattered. She was on to a good thing, and being a bright girl she knew it.

From our standpoint, that of the innocent newcomers forming their first impressions of the school, the distinction between *bumiputra* and non-*bumiputra* (which here coincided with Malay and non-Malay) was as obvious and fundamental as it was to Dr Mahathir's government, but for quite different reasons. Non-*bumi* meant friendly, *bumi* hesitant and distrustful or even downright unfriendly. Long after our arrival I talked about this with Rosniyah.

'Do you know,' she said with a trace of embarrassment, 'when the three of you first came I wanted to go and talk to you straight away, but the others – you know who I mean – they wouldn't let me. They were really shocked. They said "It's not right. You, a Muslim girl, talking to Western men! You should wait at least three weeks before you even say Good morning to them."'

The most welcoming group of people on the staff were the girls who lived in the block of school flats a couple of hundred yards across the prairie-like expanse of the playing-fields. There were four of them. Navam I have already mentioned. She was what Malays call *hitam manis*: dark and sweet. While I was still getting over my post-Fiona depression she arrived for school one morning wearing the *shalwar kameez*, the Punjabi costume: brightly-patterned baggy trousers tight at the ankles and trailing shawl. I looked up, open-mouthed, thinking for the first time what a really lovely girl she was. I had recovered.

Navamalar in Tamil means 'ninth flower'; if the ninth child had been a boy he would have been called Navaratnam, 'ninth jewel'. Navam's close friend was Teoh Kim Teng, whose name meant 'solid gold'. Kim Teng was Hakka Chinese from Penang, a tall willowy girl who ended up being given most of the girls' sports coaching to do because the Malay teachers felt it was indecorous for Muslim women to be seen leaping energetically round a netball field. Teo Choo Lay was gentle and smiling and unflappable. Ng Lee Kit was serious and a little hesitant, perhaps because she had been made head of the English department. In Malaysia this brought neither prestige, power nor extra pay, only tedious paperwork and accountability in detail for the fate of Gestetner stencils and overhead transparency markers.

They were all in their twenties, charming and vivacious and decorative girls, and looking back I am grateful to all of them. For Navam, who came from Johore, Kim Teng from Penang and Lee Kit from Kuala Lumpur the Trengganu coast was effectively almost as far from home as it was for us, and for them there was not even anything particularly exotic or interesting about it. It must have had all the appeal a small Scottish fishing town dominated by a particularly cheerless offshoot of the Free Presbyterian Church would have for a Londoner sent there against his will by Head Office. We foreigners at least had chosen to come in search of the exotic. These Malaysian commoners of the soil had not chosen to come to Trengganu, and they were all waiting eagerly for their transfer applications to be accepted by the Ministry; Malaysian education is as centralised as it is in France. We were all exiles together.

The only person whose attitude jarred, apart from those

members of the Malay staff who were either too shy, too distrustful or too disapproving to accept us, was Desmond. The two of us were sitting at a canteen table one morning when Navam and Kim Teng came down for their own coffee break. The two girls and I chatted while Desmond glared at his cup as though he suspected the presence of a cockroach in the murky depths of his coffee. After ten minutes or so Ninth Flower and Solid Gold went off to a lesson, laughing over some pleasantly silly joke. It was a bright cheerful sound in a rather joyless place, and I thought as I watched them strolling away what a nice couple of girls they were. Desmond, who had not said a word all the time, stared sullenly after them.

'Makes you sick, doesn't it?' he said. Something confiding in his tone suggested that he assumed I must feel the same, which shows how ignorant human beings can be about each other. 'What do they know about anything? They don't know a bloody thing about what it's all about. Laughing and giggling. Listen to them.'

He smiled unpleasantly. 'They'll learn.'

Desmond was only in his early thirties, but at times he could speak with all the rancid envy of a senile misanthrope. The only times I heard a note of enthusiasm creep into his voice were when he spoke about either sex or his Channel Islands savings account. He had the furtive subterranean air of a man who dissected toads for a hobby. Listening to him sometimes I used to wonder whether a career as an expatriate teacher of English was good for the soul in the long run. Travel is said to broaden the mind, but it did not seem to have done much for Desmond's.

Jim was less embittered, but he had not enjoyed his two years in Japan. He had taught in a small town, and I think the Japanese insularity towards foreigners, presumably far more obvious there than in a big city, had soured his goodwill from the start. He had come to Malaysia hoping for a more straightforward, problem-free two years, but thanks to the vacillations of the Ministry of Education he was to be disappointed.

We heard a lot about Japan. 'It must be a love-hate relationship, you know, Jim,' I said once. But Jim would not accept that love had anything to do with it.

Samuel Johnson (I was re-reading Boswell at the time) seemed to have hit the nail on the head. 'Depend upon it,' he said, 'that if a man *talks* of his misfortunes, there is something in them that is not disagreeable to him; for where there is nothing but pure misery, there never is any recourse to the mention of it.'

I used to listen to the two of them talking somtimes. They did not particularly like each other, but periodically (the school timetable being what it was) they would find themselves taking a coffee break in the canteen at the same time. What resulted as Jim's light voice with its trace of Yorkshire accent and Desmond's muddier tones overlapped with each other was conversation without communication, a kind of dissonant counterpoint, like two pieces of music in separate keys being played at the same time. It was a little like being in a music practice room with the players in the rooms to either side clearly audible, weaving their separate unrelated lines but occasionally, by coincidence, striking some bizarre passing harmony.

Each of them had one staple topic, which was the awfulness of the respective countries they had just come from (Saudi Arabia in Desmond's case), but beyond that general thematic resemblance the two monologues never really meshed with each other.

'By the time I left Yukinara, I'd just about had enough. I used to dream of going into the headmaster's office and shouting "What about the bloody Burma railroad, then, eh? Forgotten about that, have you?"'

'On Sundays they used to have public executions in the square just down the road. Imagine it.'

'And the attitude to foreigners really used to get me down. Once a *gaijin*, always a *gaijin*. Even after two years they were still pointing at me in the street.'

'I suppose it was the only kind of public entertainment they were allowed.'

'And the stress! The teachers used to hate each other. No wonder they have such a suicide rate.'

'It's not as if there's anything else to do there. No cinema, no booze.'

'Mind you, the kids are really lovely until they're about four years old. Then the thought-police get hold of them and from then on it's exams, exams, exams all the way.'

'They chop people's hands off. Really. It's true.'

'They turn their kids into zombies.'

'Or chop their heads off.'

'They never tell the truth about the war.'

'They spend their time watching blue videos, then say it's the West that's corrupt.'

'They don't want to rent you a flat if you're a foreigner.'

'And they're bloody lazy.'

'Obsessed with work.'

'Sit in an office drinking coffee all day.'

'Rushing around like mechanical toys.'

'Except when there's a beheading to watch.'

'Little tinpot dictators wanting you to show them respect all the time.'

'Hypocrites.'

'Zombies.'

'Malays are nowhere near as extreme as that.'

'No, you just have to look round the staffroom. I can't see this lot jumping out of a tenth-floor window at exam-time.'

Occasionally I used to launch into a comment myself when Desmond paused for breath, but I soon found out that he would only pause for long enough to let me get half-way through a sentence, then plough on regardless. It was like trying to manage one of those taped language drills where you have, say, precisely five seconds of recorded silence in which to gabble your response. Eventually I learned not to bother and contented myself with nodding instead. It was like living in a Dickens novel: everybody in their own world, communicating by a series of overlapping monologues.

Perhaps in self-defence, I kept a journal, which I suppose in its way was a kind of written monologue. I was following

Johnson's advice to Mrs Thrale: 'Do not remit the practice of writing down occurrences as they arise, of whatever kind. Do not omit painful casualties or unpleasing passages, they make the variegation of existence.'

Jim and I were a little uneasy at this promised invasion of Australians. There was nothing chauvinist about this attitude; the nationality of the invaders was less important than the fact that they were Westerners. It would have been the same whether they had been English or Portuguese or Norwegians or Falkland Islanders. Whatever the long shadows cast by religious disapproval or personal hygiene, we had done our best not to be stand-offish, not always to shut ourselves off in a 'Western' enclave: to be approachable but not threateningly effusive. We were aware of the dangers of huddling together into a separate corner of the staffroom, slipping into the role of the oh-so-superior foreign experts: the aid workers in the starving country gathering in the local luxury hotel.

There were occasional hitches, of course, but by and large Jim and I felt we were doing the right kind of thing, making the right kinds of noises. Now the prospect of becoming part of what amounted to a massive communal power-bloc of nine English-speaking Westerners was a little worrying. After the Malays, we would become the second largest ethnic group on the staff, outnumbering even the Chinese. At the same time we were looking forward to the human novelty of the invasion. At the very least it would add a certain 'variegation', to use Johnson's word, to canteen conversation.

My most vivid memory of the Australians' arrival is their air of almost uncontrollable energy. They seemed to leap up from their seats with startling suddenness. They rushed to unoccupied tables and began frantically scribbling material for reading comprehension or oral practice. 'Wherezatimetable?' they said. 'We'vealreadybeenherethreedaysandwehaven'tbeeninabloodyclassroomyet.'

I made soothing noises. It was my job to work out the

timetable for the nine of us, and by East Coast standards I felt I was making dizzyingly rapid progress. There were five classes getting thirty-four periods a week each, which meant a hundred and seventy slots to be filled according to a complicated formula. It took me about three days of concentrated work, on top of my own teaching, which seemed pretty good going to me considering I had never made out a timetable before and was still trying to throw off whatever bug it was that I had been incubating in the Federal Hotel.

It was a bit like watching a speeded-up film. Jim and I discussed the phenomenon. It was obviously something entirely subjective. We realised that we must have looked exactly like that ourselves to the locals when we arrived, back at the end of January: expecting teaching to start on the first day of term, expecting all the students to have arrived by the end of the first week, nervously glancing at our watches in the canteen, because we did not wish to be seen being conspicuously under-employed. We had adapted and slowed down and survived. The newcomers were still living at a different metabolic rate. It would take them about three weeks to adjust, we guessed.

They turned out to be a pleasant bunch of people, once they had acclimatised to the demands of the East Coast and slowed down to the point where I could see them clearly. There was Denis Hewett from Sydney, later to be my neighbour, who in his bearded days reminded me of the captain of a slightly disreputable coaster, a seafarer from pre-container days with a knowledge of every harbourside bar on the coast and a fund of stories to tell. John Vrachnas, Greek-Australian from Melbourne, wore a public mask of cynicism. Some of it was assumed, some of it real; it was sometimes difficult to tell which you were dealing with. Terrie (for Teresa) Ferman from Brisbane, sensitive and conscientious, was the most ladylike Australian I had ever met. 'Crass, Peter,' was her favourite judgment on the 'ocker' side of Australian life. 'Really *crass.*'

Pam and David Hagan were a teaching couple. The headmaster had been informed of this in advance, and a submerged worry surfaced on his part when I went into his office to announce the arrival of the new teachers. We arranged a time for me to escort them in for a formal introduction and allow him to make his reserved, meandering, possibly uneasy speech of welcome to them.

'I hope you will . . . remind them, Peter, not to . . . to show *any kind of affection* in public . . . the local people, you see . . . they might consider it . . . very shocking . . .'

At first you might have thought he was envisaging two people locked in a groaning embrace in the audio-visual room . . . but no. He was worried in case they might be seen holding hands as they walked out to the car park on the way home. In fact Australians are not much given as a people to extravagant displays of sentiment, so he need hardly have worried.

As far as I could work out, any kind of public affection, any indication that a private affection between the sexes exists, is seen as an appalling solecism all the way across South-East Asia. You could imagine a localised version of one of those H. M. Bateman cartoons of the thirties: THE MAN WHO SMILED AT HIS WIFE IN PUBLIC. On the other hand, Malay boys frequently walk around hand in hand well into their teens, and male teachers throw their arms round one another's shoulders and fondle one another's backs quite openly. They are not necessarily homosexuals; it is just that affection between the sexes seems to be regarded as either ridiculous or shameful, and in grossly bad taste ('crass', as Terrie Ferman would have said). It is all part of that awful business of making a fool of oneself in public which East Asians so dread: the obsession with not 'losing face'.

Affection, in Asia, is what you show to children. The widespread British lack of obvious affection towards small children strikes Asians as equally inhibited and perhaps even more disturbing. The British, of course, reserve their deepest affection for dogs, but I have said enough about them already.

The sixth of the Australians was Monica, who might have been painstakingly chosen by a malicious committee so as to shock the Malays of the East Coast to the marrow of their pious, provincial, deeply conservative being.

Monica was forty, and obsessively conscious of the fact. She was twice divorced. For a Trengganu Malay man, ironically, that would have been nothing unusual; the East Coast is said to have one of the highest divorce rates in the world. In a woman, to be divorced was invariably seen as a badge of either inadequacy, infidelity or both. She was an attractive, neurotic, maddening, oddly memorable person, with the tongue of a fishwife and the tastes of someone accustomed to cosmopolitan style and affluence. She was gloriously and worryingly out of place in Kuala Penyu with its mouldering wooden shophouses, easy pace of life and general air of being somewhere at the furthest edge of things as seen from a metropolitan perspective.

She wore neat lightweight summer frocks, and shocked the local teachers unspeakably by never bothering to wear an underskirt. She was casual in her manners but very conscious of her appearance. I never remember seeing her letting standards slip to the extent of wearing trousers; shorts I think she saw as an abomination. She had two small boys who had been expensively educated in Australia at some 'enlightened' private school on the lines of A. S. Neill's Summerhill. She hated the thought of having their individuality cramped at State schools. Whether because of this expensive neglect or not, Matthew and Justin were universally dreaded in Malaysia as destructive undisciplined little monsters.

Her figure was trim, her voice harsh, modulating into something pleading when she wanted someone to do her a favour, which was most of the time. She smoked heavily, and made disbelieving, scornful, unprintable comments when a message was relayed in school (deviously as usual, through Rosniyah) that it was not acceptable for a woman to smoke in the school canteen, even in the privacy of the enclosed section. Nobody minded about men. She had enormous charm and yet drove people to fury because she always tried to extract more and more from them, as though driven by some sort of compulsion, like a kleptomaniac. With a mixture of wheedling charm, slyness and a kind of suppressed hysteria she went from acquaintance to acquaintance trying to persuade someone else to prop her life up for her, to look after her children or take over her lessons for the day.

To use a rather discredited word, she was triumphantly and undilutedly feminine, which did not mean she was in any sense soft. She had the single-minded ruthlessness of the totally self-absorbed.

Monica was a difficult person to talk to because it was impossible to avoid saying the wrong thing to her sooner or later. She called in to see me once to ask about ways of travelling down to Singapore for the long weekend holiday which was coming up.

'I can't face driving that far. What do you think about going down by bus?'

'You could. Santanara Express. I went down by share-taxi myself last time, though. It's a bit quicker. Change at Kuantan and you can get one all the way to Mersing.'

Monica's blue eyes opened wide in horror. 'But those *drivers!*' she said in her nicotine-sandpapered voice. 'I'd be sick with fear and worry in case we *crashed!*'

She leaned forward and looked into my eyes. Her voice sank to its wheedling alternative tone. She said with an air of intense seriousness: 'Tell me, Peter – I'd be safer in a bus, wouldn't I?'

Sometimes the charm worked, and you found yourself playing along with what Monica wanted. At other times you found yourself reacting against what felt like manipulation. This was one of those other times.

'If you're concerned about road safety in this country I wouldn't have said there's a lot to choose between bus drivers and taxi drivers. They're all lunatics. On the other hand if anything did happen, I suppose a bus would be higher off the ground.'

'Oh my *God*,' said Monica in a voice as harsh as a seabird's. Her expression was appalled. She stopped trying to wheedle; it was as though a mask had slipped askew. 'Jesus, all I'm fucking trying to do is get down to stinking fucking Singapore. You wouldn't think it was much to ask.'

'Well then, take a bus as far as Kuantan and fly. I think there's a flight a couple of times a week. Maybe more.'

She looked at me with theatrical disbelief, as though I had suggested riding pillion with a motorcycle gang. '*Flying?* I never. Never. Fly. You may call me neurotic. I know I am. I know it. You don't need to tell me that. I admit it. I'm neurotic. But if there is any alternative I never. Ever. Fly. And now you've left me twice as bloody neurotic as when I came.'

Jim had bought a small second-hand black-and-white television. We were watching it together one evening over a gin-and-tonic when Monica arrived. She had already had several drinks and was in a self-unburdening mood.

'Jim . . . may I ask you a personal question? How old are you? Thirty? What about you, Peter?'

I calculated quickly. 'In ten days' time I'll be thirty-nine.'

There was a sudden *clunk* as Monica put down the glass Jim had given her. 'But you can't be. You're only a year short of me, and you look bloody *years* younger.'

She put her head to one side and lowered her voice to its wheedling be-a-gentleman-and-tell-the-girl-what-she-wants-to-believe tone. 'Tell me, Peter: I don't look forty, do I? Real-lee?'

'Well, I wouldn't worry, Monica, you certainly don't look any older.'

Monica collapsed. 'God!' she said in a bird-like croak. 'I suppose that means I don't look any bloody younger. That does it. I'm going to get my bloody face lifted.'

What I wanted to tell her, but could see no way of managing, was that yes, she did look forty, but an attractive forty. And there are no face-lifts in the world that will make a woman of forty into an innocent young girl. In the way she talked, in her savage wit, her knowingness, her cynicism, her occasional outbursts of devastating bitterness, a varied experience of life with two husbands in at least four countries came through, like the taste of garlic in good cooking. It was one of the things which made her attractive. But I knew when to keep my mouth shut. I had been well-tutored by Fiona.

The Australians had seven school-age children between them. The arrangement with the company had been that education would be provided for all those children, which was why Denis, John, Terrie, Pam, David and Monica had been posted to the same town. Terrie's husband, confusingly also called Dennis (Dennis Castles), had been engaged to teach the seven children. Dennis Castles had a brooding look, a little like the poet Ted Hughes, and a deadpan way of talking which depended strongly on a single expletive. I have an early memory of bumping into him in the main street of the town. It was in the middle of the day and the sun was hot. Later he and Terrie were to buy a battered second-hand Volvo, but at the time he was on a bicycle, looking decidedly pink.

'Jeez, I feel awful. I met these fuckin' Indians from KL, here on a contract. Electricians. They took me out and got me fuckin' drunk. I said, 'Saya mesti fuckin' pergi,' and they said. 'No, you stay and fuckin' drink.' And with fuckin' visitors coming an' all. Jeez, what a state to be in.'

'Bit hot to be riding that thing,' I said.

Dennis had once worked in a mine somewhere in the desert interior of Queensland. He waved a hand airily. Sweat dripped from his jutting chin.

'Compared with outback Queensland,' he said, 'this is fuckin' temperate.' I watched him cycle unsteadily on in the direction of the town centre.

The conversation among a group of us once turned to Australian attitudes towards the sun; the only Australian religion, someone said, was sun-worship. Dennis Castles pointed to a tiny depression on his nose, the sort of scar which a long-forgotten boil might leave behind it: scarcely more than a pockmark.

'Skin cancer,' he said, as off-handedly as though he were

talking about blackheads. 'They freeze 'em off with liquid fuckin' nitrogen. Come to Queensland, the Sunshine State. Melanoma capital of the fuckin' world.'

Eventually your ears accustomed themselves to Dennis's standard expletive (which I think he was scarcely aware of using most of the time, like language teachers who say 'OK?' twice in every sentence). Terrie made determined efforts to prod him in the direction of respectability from time to time, to no avail. The expletives (which only came out when he was dealing with adults) obscured the fact that he was by all accounts a brilliant primary teacher. He had limitless reserves of patience: that tough, profane, unshockable equanimity which is the single most attractive Australian quality. Even Monica's two little monsters Matthew and Justin began to reveal unsuspected burgeonings of humanity after a month or two in the 'school' which was no more than one end of Terrie and Dennis's little seaside bungalow.

He was also an amazing raconteur, with a fund of dryly humorous, scarcely believable anecdotes told in a rapid-fire deadpan voice which had that curious Australian way of going up in intonation at the end of a sentence, like this? As though you were always being invited to make a comment? Or give encouragement?

I tried to note down one of Dennis Castles's stories, but trying to retell it I find it falls apart in my hands. Like all the best raconteurs he had a way of making the most unlikely things seem totally convincing, as though he really had spent years in some part of the world where events and human eccentricities loomed larger and more bizarre than anything in what most of us think of as life.

I remembered Cyril in the Ship restaurant in Kuala Lumpur with his sparkler. That was tame stuff in comparison with the New Zealander in Dennis's story who had exploded fireworks at parties, inside his house as well as outside. Not content with making sure his parties went with a bang, he used to hide a cylinder of nitrous oxide in a corner of the room behind a curtain. Unaware that they were inhaling laughing gas the guests would be kept in fits of hysterics as Catherine wheels and Roman candles flared, roared and zooshed around them.

'It got pretty destructive of property, but the bloke didn't mind. It was like a spectacular, he had to have a new special effect every time. People got to expect it. One day the guests were all standing happily talking to each other when suddenly – *whoomp!* – a whole fuckin' side wall came crashing in on to the floor. The bloke had got a couple of guys with chain-saws to stand outside and cut the edge of the wall, then push. Jeez, can you imagine the shock?'

At this point the authorities intervened. The armoury of fireworks kept inside the house, they said, constituted a menace to public safety, especially in a country of wooden houses like New Zealand. He was told he would have to find proper storage for the fireworks inside one of the concrete bunkers used for storing industrial explosives. Apparently the daily rates for this kind of storage are exorbitant. But the inventiveness of a man who could rig up a supply of laughing-gas and a self-destructing house wall to keep his party guests amused was not to be defeated by a technicality like this.

'Bloke went for a walk not long after that, saw this patch of derelict land on the edge of town. It gave him an idea. He bought it and built a storage bunker of his own on it. From then on he was sitting pretty. He rented out extensions of it to other people who needed a place to store their fuckin' gelignite. Made a good living too. Firework parties every week after that. Richest fuckin' pyromaniac in the world. Laughing all the way to the bunker.'

Tinggol

There are moments of claustrophobia in any small town. Aside from the ways of escape offered by the Forest Reserve and the main road which led northwards to Kuala Trengganu and southwards to Kuantan, I used to find myself lured in two directions. One was inland, following the course of the Penyu river in imagination into the forested hills of the interior. The other was seawards, towards the twin-humped silhouette of Pulau Tinggol on the horizon. Malaysia's offshore islands are among the world's most beautiful, and the East Coast has far more than its fair share of them. Some, like Tioman to the south, off Mersing in Johore, have been to some extent developed for tourism. Others, like Tinggol, or Kapas thirty miles to the north, are uninhabited and undeveloped. They are vehicles for pure romantic escape.

Kapas was the smaller and more accessible of the two. You reached it by taking a boat from the straggling village of Marang on a flat sandy strip of coast dense with coconut palms. Jim and I took a boat across one blazing day in May, with the sky a dazzling blue in all directions except inland, where you could see the white cumulus clouds boiling up like milk in preparation for a late-afternoon downpour.

The island was about a mile and a half long, gently hilly, its coastline broken up into a series of short sandy beaches with rocky headlands at either end and a scrambling, engulfing mass of vegetation screening the forested interior. On the far side, facing the open sea, there were high grey cliffs and woods blown and deformed by wind and salt spray like a memory of the Pembrokeshire or Cornish coast on the stormy Atlantic fringes of Britain.

We snorkelled from a secluded bay, admiring tiny brilliant fish and evil-looking blue masses of sea-urchin spines. The beach was littered with broken fragments of dead coral like sponge-textured branches, white as bone. I have a large piece on a bookshelf here in Brunei, where I am writing this. It looks like a warty parody of a skull. A solitary mud-wasp has built her nursery on the baroque protrusions of its surface, so that the white coral looks as though it had sprouted a massive clay-coloured carbuncle. From this, some day, the adult wasp will tunnel its way out.

Looking towards the island as I floated on my back I could see a scattering of mop-headed coconut palms leaning over the low trees whose glossy leaves sheltered a narrow strip of

the beach from the midday sun. In the opposite direction, not more than a quarter of a mile off the north end of the island, was a tiny islet only a few hundred yards long. Far beyond that a conical summit was dimly visible. I knew this was Pulau Bidong, the island the Malaysians use as a transit camp for the Vietnamese boat-people who are washed up on their coast.

It was only when I looked at a map of the whole region that I realised how close that southernmost peninsula of Vietnam, west of the Mekong delta, comes to Malaysia. Bear in mind that from November to February or thereabouts a powerful wind blows from the north-east, and it is clear why that part of the South China Sea is a graveyard for Vietnamese refugees and the coast of Kelantan and Trengganu a frequent point of landfall for those who survive. Kuala Penyu is less than three hundred miles from the far south of Vietnam, as close as the regional metropolis of Singapore, as close as Cornwall or Newcastle to London. More than once I had seen the burnt-out black skeletons of refugee boats half-burned in the sand without realising what they were.

Months later, passing the grove of tall feathery casuarina trees behind the beach at Telok Lipat, I saw a great gaggle of people watching the beach. A square of this had been cordoned off like a boxing ring, and in this enclosure fifteen or twenty Vietnamese men and women were sitting blankly or sprawled asleep on the sand. They were in their twenties, with a ragged unkempt gipsyish look about them, which was hardly surprising considering they might have been at sea for a week or two. There were armed Malay soldiers sitting on the rocks nearby.

'*Orang Vietnam?*' I asked one of them.

He grunted.

'*Di mana kapal?* Where is the boat?'

He grunted again. I was not going to learn much from official sources.

The boat turned out to be a little way along the beach. It was twenty or twenty-five feet long, and I cannot say much about its construction because when I saw it, not much more than twenty-four hours after its arrival, it was already a smouldering hulk. I was puzzled by the waste at first, but I suppose if twenty seasick people have been using a confined space as many feet long as a latrine for two weeks it is understandable that nobody should be enthusiastic about refitting it.

It was a still, diamond-clear evening. Dusk was just falling, with successive waves inching at their leisure up the beach to lap at the boat's blackened stern. Along one side the wood was still glowing red. I could smell it burning; the smoke was aromatic, with the sandalwood smell of the driftwood logs people burned on the beach. The propeller had been taken, but the engine was still in place.

Later I learned that the refugees had been taken off to Pulau Bidong. They had been fed by the Red Crescent, and by all accounts they had looked happy as they set off up the coast road. I hoped that their luck would hold. To have survived the murdering rapists of the Gulf of Thailand was something. In another sense their Odyssey was only just beginning.

Kapas was only a half-hour trip from the harbour at Marang. Tinggol, larger and much higher but also uninhabited, was directly off Kuala Penyu but four times the distance from the coast. Unlike Kapas, which was a regular excursion destination for local people and hence could get crowded at holiday weekends, Tinggol (I hope the present tense is still accurate) is not on any regular excursion or tourist route. As a result there was much more of a feeling of accomplishment about getting there.

For the first time I found myself part of a large travelling group, which made a change from pretending to be Robinson Crusoe. Denis Hewett, playing the part of the bearded sea-captain to perfection, had chartered a fishing-boat. All the Australians came with the exception of Monica who said it sounded like her idea of Purgatory and took the day off instead. A New Zealand couple from Johore and an Anglo-French family from Kuantan drove up for the day, together with Stuart Robertson whom I had not seen since the fiasco at the Federal Hotel nearly six months before. Altogether, including Desmond, Jim and myself, there were about twenty of us. The scene at the dilapidated Nibong Quay, a mile up the estuary, was like one of those Victorian paintings of emigrants leaving Britain: bags and boxes and children everywhere.

There was no shelter on the boat except for the couple of seats next to the helmsman in the small cabin, so we arranged ourselves on available patches of deck as best we could, leaning against the gunwales. The early morning sky was clear as we moved down the estuary to the sound of a chugging diesel engine, but as it turned out the day was only occasionally sunny thanks to thin veils of cloud. Which was just as well, or we would have come back as red as lobsters. Three of the children sat up above the cabin keeping watch for sharks (no confirmed sightings) and particularly large approaching waves (frequent). Occasionally we would see a flying-fish skittering across the surface, then burrowing into an approaching wave. They were smaller than I had imagined. One adult and one child were sick on the way. We had got off lightly.

The final stage of the approach, as the boat moved gently across the sheltered bay to the quay which faced the distant mainland, was the quintessence of tropical island fantasy: a curve of beach, backed by low thick-leaved trees, with a wall of forest rearing behind to twin peaks. The higher of these, which rose sheer behind the beach to a flat summit, must have been about a thousand feet high.

There was fresh water from a couple of wells near the island's only quay, but no settlement. The air of total lack of habitation was faintly marred by a couple of tents which had been set up further along the beach by a sub-aqua club from Singapore. On the other hand, nobody but a desert-island fanatic (there are such people) could have denied that there was room for all of us: even for the seven energetic children, who in this setting of other-worldly calm were remarkably free from tantrums and tears.

Island-hopping in company may not be the experience of self-discovery travelling on your own can be, but on a human level it is far more enjoyable. Instead of being lulled (or forced) into introspection and the kind of close, slightly jaundiced observation beloved of solitary travellers, you have the chance to swap some potato salad or an egg mayonnaise sandwich for a piece of chicken at lunch-time. Meanwhile beside you a group of Australians – brought up from childhood on the ritual of the backyard barbie and the Esky full of cool tubes, as their English counterparts are brought up on the corresponding ritual of the country walk in the rain and the return to indoor warmth and hot buttered toast – brew up the billy on a paraffin stove. There are worse ways of spending a Saturday.

The only disenchanting element of the whole trip was the journey back. Even on the way out the swell had been noticeable, but at four o'clock it was decidedly rougher. White horses were more in evidence than flying-fish, and a stiff breeze blew spray in drifts over the side as the boat dipped and rose. The cloud-cover had thickened, obscuring every trace of the sun. Sitting huddled under a towel at the edge of the deck, soaking wet, I realised for the first time that it is perfectly possible to feel cold when you are only five degrees from the equator.

The intellectual excitement of this discovery did not last for long. I was shivering uncontrollably when we reached the quay on the Penyu estuary at the end of the two-hour journey. The emigrants, a trifle subdued, unloaded their belongings. One or two faces were tinged with green. Visitors were assigned to this or that house to stay the night.

'Oh, by the way, Peter,' said Denis Hewett, not meeting my eyes, 'I've – um – put Stuart Robertson in with you. Hope that's all right.'

I was not enthusiastic, but it seemed a pity to spoil a good excursion by throwing a tantrum at the end of it. Surely, I reasoned as I heard my teeth chattering, the man would have adjusted to life alongside other people by now. All that quarrelsomeness at the Federal Hotel had probably just been a bad case of culture-shock. And surely by now he must have learned to stop talking, at least now and then. I hoped he would have the decency to be as exhausted as I was after an afternoon's swimming and four hours on an uncomfortable boat.

Stuart, perhaps hardened by generations of Pictish or Celtic ancestors with only smouldering peat fires to keep out the damp chill of the Highlands, did not appear to be feeling the cold. I heated enough water in the electric kettle to be able to sluice a bucketful over myself, draped myself in a towelling dressing-gown I had always previously found too hot to wear in that climate (outside the fierce air-conditioning of the Federal Hotel) and made scalding coffee for both of us. Stuart gave me a fresh half-hour rundown on the various teaching projects he had been in charge of during his career, in case I had not heard properly last time, or forgotten.

I nodded frequently (the exercise helped to warm me up) and began to feel physically restored. There was something pleasantly, drowsily hypnotic about listening to Stuart's murmuring well-bred gabble. At least I was not being expected to say anything. Vague dream-like memories of an open boat and an uncomfortable journey through tropical waters alive with flying-fish drifted through my mind as I listened to this apparently endless monologue. It was all rather like the story of the Ancient Mariner, but jumbled.

Suddenly Stuart's voice faded like a feeble BBC World Service signal overtaken by atmospherics. His eyes glittered.

'Ah, Peter. I don't think I've had a chance to try my lateral thinking puzzles on you yet. I've got a collection of thirty-seven so far. Just try this one to start with . . .'

I surfaced with a start. It was too much. I jumped from my chair and switched on the radio-cassette-player. Gabbling as the Wedding-Guest must have, I said: 'That reminds me, Stuart, I bought a handful of pirated cassettes when I was in Singapore a couple of weeks ago. This is Mozart. Piano concertos. Daniel Barenboim. I think it's pretty good.'

The sound of an orchestra filled the room, and I subsided with relief into my armchair. You had to be devious in the East now and then, I thought to myself. Who said Westerners were always direct and straightforward? I saw Stuart's mouth opening and closing, a shifting cultivator's clearing within the *belukar* of his beard, then closed my eyes and drifted away with Mozart.

PULAU KAPAS

They spell adventure, these little islands:
Just as much as you can safely manage.
Kapas even has a smaller one in tow:
One beach, two rocks, five coconut-palms
    And a whale-sized wood.

Kapas has an interior, too, where sudden
Birds call in the cool laurel woods,
And you can pretend the red flower you find
(Doubtless a common weed of tropical coasts)
    Is new to science.

Or you can clamber over rocks from one
Bay to another, then in the translucent
Shallows swim past coral, darting fish,
Sea-slugs, and spiny poisonous horrors
  (Which can be avoided).

You can play games, in fact, content to wade
Through the warm shallows of Kapas, unaware
Of that grey hump in the distance where the haunted
Vietnamese in their camp remember a grimmer
  Kind of adventure.

The River

Nibong Quay, where we had embarked for Tinggol, looked like a relic from the days of Joseph Conrad. Various rotting or rusting hulks lay around on the tidal mud, and the wooden supports of the quay itself looked as though a heavy job of unloading would bring the whole ramshackle structure down. Across the river was a line of low woodland with coconut palms prominent here and there. On sandbanks where fishing-boats lay beached were ancient coconuts, dried and weathered, looking like grey skulls.

    You very rarely saw any activity at Nibong Quay, except in the form of a few small boys fishing or bathing in the river. Despite, or perhaps because of, this air of disuse and dilapidation, I found it an evocative place. Ever since my teens I had been haunted by the idea of travelling up a jungle river. Where I had got the image from I do not know, but in my imagination it had involved dense trees overhanging the water, monkeys in the branches and parrots flashing overhead, a dilapidated boat with a seedy captain: a journey into mysterious darkness, an atmosphere which was a cross between the sinister, the bizarre and the enticing. At university I read Conrad's *Heart of Darkness*, but was selfishly disappointed to find that it was not the world of my own fantasy. Now, more years later than I cared to think, to find myself beside this slow brown tropical estuary was to feel I was in a dream which was in the process of coming true. There were no parrots in Malaysia, it was true, but the rest of the paraphernalia was there waiting for me.

It helped to make up for the idiocies of school life, for the feeling of isolation which sometimes came painfully to the fore, for the discomforts of 4F-1 Jalan Nibong with its outside privy, its absence of hot water beyond what could be heated in an electric kettle, its ridiculous aluminium-painted interior, the noise of my neighbours. These things I endured, just as Londoners endure the grimy discomfort of commuting daily on the Underground. Amid all this, the river – even more than the beach or the islands – was a constant reminder that something like a current of mystery still managed to run through it all. It was a Wind-in-the-Willows fascination and a haunting landscape of the mind at the same time.

I found it hard to imagine what sort of hinterland the river flowed from. As far as I could tell from maps of the country, human settlement in the state of Trengganu was almost entirely limited to the coastal strip. Townships of some kind were marked inland at Jerangau and Kuala Brang and the isolated iron-mining settlement of Batu Besi, but that was about all. Along the flat coast road, behind the casuarinas and coconut palms and Indian almond trees of the beach, the straggling wooden kampongs seemed to merge with one another in a kind of ribbon development, but inland there appeared to be next to nothing. To travel by road across the peninsula you first had to go ninety miles down the coast to Kuantan, from which the direct road led to Kuala Lumpur. There was a so-called East-West Highway under construction, but it was right up near the Thai border, more than twice as far away. This left a substantial part of the State marked on the map as completely roadless. There were precious few ways of travelling even five miles into the interior. It all aroused a certain curiosity.

When a couple of girls teaching in Kuantan came up to stay with Jim for the weekend, the four of us drove inland along the Jerangau road to see what we could find. Past the malodorous rubbish-tip on the edge of the Bukit Bauk Forest Reserve we crested a rise and drove on past scrubby hills and the occasional padi-field, beneath a dramatic cumulus sky.

I used to try to work out why it was that a sky like this, the kind you might see in an English summer – drifting galleons of bosomy cumulus with wisps of high-altitude cirrus against the blue – looked so recognisably different in the humid tropics. Partly, I suppose, it was the sheer intensity of the light. It also had to do with the same impression you got from the leaves of trees. The trees themselves often looked surprisingly like familiar temperate broadleaf species, elms or sycamores or limes or alders, in overall outline, except that in general they grew taller. But there was a certain tough sun-hardened quality in the evergreen leaves that you would not find in their Northern European equivalents: like the chitinous wing-cases of beetles. The clouds were a parallel case: the familiar billows of cumulus, but more definite in shape, harder and more waxy and more durable-looking, as though they had been injected with silicone.

The hills rose higher. We were beyond the limits of the Forest Reserve by now, but there was still plenty of primary forest left unlogged. A few miles further on was the hamlet of Jerangau, and here, for the first time since the vicinity of Nibong Quay, the road met the Penyu river. At the top of a steep bank a Rose of India tree – *Lagerstroemia* – was a mass of intensely mauve flowers, startling amid the unrelieved green of the forest's edge. There was no other road marked on the map, but we decided to chance our luck down a small unmarked (though metalled) lane signposted in Malay WATER PURIFICATION WORKS.

The road led us over a rickety wooden bridge, then

snaked on through forest and the occasional rubber plantation. After a few miles the tarmac came to an end and we found ourselves bumping over an unmetalled surface of red laterite. We were close to the river again, and the views were memorable, particularly when the road rose a hundred feet or so above the brown river with its strips of white sandbank. Swathes of creeper hung from the ragged domes of the trees behind like half-raised curtains in front of a stage, and behind these in turn the forested hills rolled away into the distance to where the highlands of the interior showed purple glimpses through heaped-up masses of cloud which looked as substantial as whipped cream.

At the end of the laterite road, about thirty miles inland, we came to a riverside Malay village called Kuala Jengai. There was no fridge in the village and hence no ice for soft drinks, so we sat outside the one café and drank sweet milkless tea, which would have been more refreshing if there had been a lime to be bought anywhere in this uninspiring hamlet. Half the village children turned out to watch us in blank unsmiling silence. They had a faintly inbred look.

I had been reading *The Malay Dilemma*, the remarkable book written by Dr Mahathir Mohamad back in 1970. Until he became Prime Minister it was banned. Had it been written by anyone other than a Malay it could easily be seen as a monument to anti-Malay racism because of a certain underlying attitude which emerges in the course of the book. Although Mahathir dislikes the British and distrusts the Chinese he is at least prepared to grant them both some grudging respect for their accomplishments. Towards his own people he is merciless as he describes the passivity and fatalism of the rural Malays, their inability to enter into the money economy. When he praises the coastal urban Malays, with their admixture of blood over the centuries from Indian and Arab traders, as having more enterprise and grasp of economic reality, you remember that Mahathir himself is half-Kerala-Indian.

But his picture of the unleavened inland Malays – with the inbreeding and genetic degeneration which he sees as resulting from the Muslim insistence on everyone, even the retarded, marrying and having children – is rather shocking. Kuala Jengai struck me as the sort of community Mahathir saw, fairly or otherwise, as an albatross round the neck of Malay advancement.

At peak viewing time there were twenty-five people, adults as well as children, watching us in a semi-circle as we drank our not-particularly-refreshing tea. It was disconcerting, more so than the normal smiling curiosity of Malay children which annoys newcomers but which residents come to enjoy. 'The arrival of strangers at a place so rarely visited' (Samuel Johnson writing about a visit to the Isle of Skye) 'excites rumour, and quickens curiosity.' In this case it may be that the abbreviated shorts Valerie and Carole were wearing had something to do with the quickened curiosity.

On the way back we picnicked on a riverside sandbank. 'Look,' said Val, smiling, 'crocodile tracks!' In fact they had been made by a large monitor lizard. The silence was loud with cicades and the rippling of the current. As we listened, lulled into an afternoon trance, there came the bubbling mysterious call of a bulbul, that most breathtaking of all South-East Asian songbirds. Listening to it, looking up at the spindly rattan vines twisting up through the trees to where their topmost fronds curled delicately against the sky like feathers, I knew that I wanted, most than almost anything else, to find some way of travelling further upriver.

After only a couple of weeks, quite unexpectedly, my wish came true. Shortly after the drive to Kuala Jengai, a notice in Malay went up on the staffroom notice-board at school. BERAKIT KE HULU PENYU, it said. The line after this appeared to say 'Hunting, shooting and fishing.' I knew that *hulu* or *ulu* meant the upper river, the headwaters, hence by extension the interior, the backwoods, the boondocks. I had an idea that *rakit* meant raft. A raft-trip to the Upper Penyu river? It sounded intriguing but unsafe.

I fetched my dictionary to check. On the way to *rakit* I was sidetracked (as one always is sidetracked in dictionaries) by *rubing*, because on the basis of the definition given it seemed to epitomise the kind of word which must have typified the Malay language before the *Dewan Bahasa dan Pustaka*, the Government-controlled Institute for Language and Literature, decided to transform it. The language of concrete village reference with its wealth of pithy proverbs, spoken by rice-farmers and fishermen, had been ripped apart to make way for the abstractions and intellectual fashions of Western-style thought. Like a sleepy provincial town gutted to make room for office blocks, air-conditioned shopping centres and multi-storey local government headquarters, it now bristled with words like *Saintifik* and *Teknologi* and *Fizik Atomik* and *Agregit* and *Nasionalisme*. Sometimes the Malay schoolchildren were as lost in it as any foreigner.

Here, though, I was back in the world of traditional kampong Malay. '*Rubing*,' said the dictionary, 'a temporary light gunwale to increase the freeboard of a Malay boat; the wash-strake.'

It occurred to me that I would not have known a washstrake if a paranoiac fisherman had swung one at my head. And yet I was teaching children most of whom came from the rural, deeply traditional states of Kelantan and Trengganu, many of whom must have been far more at home in boats bristling with wash-strakes than they were in the classroom struggling with *Fizik* and *Teknologi*. Beside them, I was the ignorant one. What did I know except my own language and the jargon that goes with teaching it? If I really wanted to go up the Penyu river into the *ulu*, knowing about wash-strakes would have been a great deal more useful than knowing the difference between a long open question and a short closed one, or being able to utter a velar plosive on request.

I went to ask Rosniyah's friend Cikgu Anisah, the Malay teacher, about *berakit*, but before I could reach her desk there was a disturbance. The *ustaz* Musa, in a state of high excitement, burst into the staffroom with his hands raised to heaven and his voice aggrieved. Words of denunciation poured out. I heard *Saya tahu* – 'I know' – and frequent appeals to *Allah*. He moved with animation from one Malay teacher to another, taking them by the shoulders or the ears and shaking them. They lowered their gaze, sheepish and embarrassed. The non-Muslim staff, knowing themselves to be mercifully excluded from this, gave one another meaningful looks and the trace of a smile.

I thought at the time that the *ustaz* was having some kind of fit, but Navam and a new young Chinese teacher called Sharon explained things to me afterwards. As I had been vaguely aware, a group of official speakers had come earlier that morning to give the students a talk on *Amanah Saham Nasional*, the *bumiputra*-only savings scheme which the Government was concerned to spread as widely as possible: the one which paid seventeen per cent interest, but only to the princes and princesses of the soil. What I had been watching was a microcosm of the difficulties the Government was having in its attempt to encourage gung-ho consumer-driven economic growth in the face of rearguard action by the Islamic fundamentalists, who had been coming out of the woodwork ever since the Iranian revolution.

Dr Mahathir's government made a point of playing the Islamic card as often as possible, preaching 'Islamic values' to the people and founding an Islamic bank so as to out-manoeuvre the fundamentalists. But Islam forbids the payment of interest, defining it as usury (just as the Catholic church used to), and the *ustaz* was pointing this out to the Muslim teachers in no uncertain terms. By having anything to do with this scheme, he was saying, you are defiling yourselves. By not making your opposition to it known, you are encouraging others to defile themselves. The only kind of interest which should matter to you is the interest a virtuous soul earns, year by year, in the sight of God.

Apparently (I was sorry to have missed this) he had even disrupted the talk that morning by shouting the speakers down, which seemed to me a remarkably un-Malay thing to do. It was all a bit like Mr Paisley at the European Parliament during an official welcome for the Pope.

I was right about *rakit*, but with the prefix it turned out to mean a river-trip in general. This one (it took place a week later) was a group excursion with a vengeance; thirty of us jammed ourselves into the school minibus which was to take us as far as Kuala Jengai, following the route Jim, Val, Carole and I had taken a couple of weeks before. Wedged between our belongings – the emigrants were leaving by bus this time – we bumped across the precarious wooden bridge at Jerangau and on to the red dirt road. From the crest of a hill I glimpsed the brown river winding through dense primary forest and felt a ridiculous sense of anticipation, as though I were a child again in Dorset being taken on an excursion to what seemed to me mysterious and alluring places like Hambledon Hill or Badbury Rings or the Isle of Purbeck.

The boats we boarded at Kuala Jengai were narrow thirty-footers with a long metal canopy on a precarious-looking frame and a powerful outboard motor. We sped on, hugging our knees, between high forested hills. For much of the journey huge *neram* trees leaned steeply over the river, so that it was like passing under endless broken archways. Their root-systems dominated the dense vegetation of the bank. A blue kingfisher flashed across the river, and monkeys watched us from the base of a tree. On one sandbank a large monitor lizard lay sunning itself.

At the camp-site the Malay teachers leapt into action, hacking saplings and lengths of bamboo into forked poles to support a gigantic tarpaulin shelter. The small group of Westerners, happy to leave the display of woodcraft to the locals, swam or tried to swing from the lianas which hung into the water from the wall of trees opposite, but these turned out to be too rotten to bear even a well-fed monkey, much less Tarzan of the Apes.

We were getting hungry. I waded out of the river and idly explored the undergrowth for a few minutes before I walked the few yards back to the camp. A small friendly teacher called Kamaruddin with a wide smile and no front teeth pointed at my leg. '*Pacat*,' he said.

'*Pacat?*'

I looked down. I had acquired my first leech, as well as a new Malay word. The leech was plump and brown, about half an inch long. I scraped it off with a certain satisfaction. This too was part of the experience.

I would not myself have brought a massive pot of rice to cook when camping in the jungle, but this was Asia, and as Asians are never tired of telling you, they do not feel properly full after a meal unless they have eaten a plateful of rice. With the rice was a curry made with tinned sardines and *ikan bilis* which are tiny dried fish undercooked, in this case, so that they resembled shreds of fish-flavoured leather bootlace, together with sweet potatoes and sweetcorn roasted on the fire. After the sun had gone down we sat talking round the campfire by dramatic moonlight, with great clear-edged clouds overhead. So far the weather had been perfect.

It was too perfect to last. Around half-past nine it started to rain, and we all retreated under the enormous open-sided tent. The rain grew heavier. Denis Hewett, John Vrachnas and I cleared trenches in the sand with our bare hands to keep the rivulets of water from invading our sleeping-space. I made sure all my belongings were safely tied up inside plastic bags and then fell asleep regardless of the rain.

Denis had his twelve-year-old son Ben with him, John had his nine-year-old daughter Heidi. We were all cramped together at one end of the tent, and it may have been the children's elbows which kept the two parents awake. Unencumbered, I slept far better than I had expected, considering that the rain must have been blowing and dripping in for at least a couple of hours, the floor was bare riverside sand and I had only a tee-shirt, a wet pair of jeans and a cotton sarong to keep me warm.

I woke at six-thirty into a world shrouded magically in mist. We had camped at the confluence of a tributary with the main river, and I wandered up this side-stream to relieve myself amid the obscured grey outlines of the dawn forest. From far off came the calls of monkeys and a deep grunting which I took to be wild boar. The tributary was a clearwater stream, the first I had seen in that part of the world, rippling briskly over a bed of stones. I lay down in it bodily, enjoying this moment of solitude, and thought how unbelievably lucky I was, in a world of wage-slavery, ideological obsession and galloping consumer greed, to be able to spend even a short time in the intricate, breathtaking, inexhaustible world of the rain-forest.

The tall pale-trunked trees across the river began to loom more clearly out of the mist. I clambered naked out of the stream and towelled myself vigorously with my sarong. It was like being present at the dawn of the world.

Meanwhile life, as usual, was ambling on in the direction of anti-climax, like a donkey which has spied a particularly succulent clump of thistles across the meadow. I strolled back to camp just in time to see shrouded figures beginning to stir. I heard Denis's voice groaning: 'I never want to live through another night like that again.' At the same moment one of the local teachers turned the radio on for the early news. We heard a report in Malay, which I dare say would have been interesting enough to those it concerned, about a mini-estate project in Kedah. Later, at intervals, we were treated to a series of repetitions of a particularly inane Malay pop cassette. Obviously the locals were not interested in the mystery and wonder of the rain-forest at dawn.

Driven out of Eden by an angel with a flaming transistor radio, I joined the others for breakfast with the wild noises shut safely out and the river-mist dissolving into the blue, white and gold sky of a tropical dawn.

There had been very little heavy rain for several weeks (though after the previous night you could have fooled us), and the depleted river grew increasingly shallow as we ascended. Once or twice we had to get out to help push the boat over the pebbles of the shallows. It was a slow business, and when signs of settlement began to appear several of us left the boat altogether. We were nearing our destination, an isolated village called Pasir Raja – Kingsand – and a rural footpath offered a short cut across the neck of a large loop in the river. We walked on a couple of miles towards Pasir Raja beneath betel-nut palms, durian and rambutan trees.

The neatness of this rural enclave in the rain-forest was surprising. Allowing for the difference in the vegetation it was like the well-tended countryside around an English village. Kuala Jengai had seemed down-at-heel and inbred, but this was a Home Counties kind of kampong, a world away from the scruffy, littered fishing settlements of Seberang Pintasan on the far side of the river-mouth. It was odd to think that we were now deep in the interior of the country, almost at the head of navigation, with the uninhabited highlands of Taman Negara, the peninsular National Park, looming ahead of us.

High up on those forested slopes was the white gash of a waterfall. The midday sun was blazing down, and our little group of pedestrian stragglers began to flag. By now the path had led us back to the river, and through the screening trees we suddenly caught sight of the unladen boat, with only the two boatmen in it, moving past us up-river. Whooping and shouting we ran down to catch it. What did it matter if we had to get out every few hundred yards and wade knee-deep beside it? At least it would be cool.

In fact it mattered a great deal to my feet, which took a long time to recover from stumbling across endless river-bed stones. Too late I realised why experienced up-river travellers brought an extra pair of canvas shoes with them.

At Pasir Raja we had a late lunch by the riverside. 'Not sardines *again* . . .' said the two Australian children. But the monotony of the sardine curry was varied by halved hard-boiled duck-eggs, acquired locally, and there was fresh coconut water to drink: cool, barely sweet and with a trace of saltiness, one of the most delicious of all drinks on a hot afternoon. After the rice had been devoured I produced the last of my tea-bags and found to my delight that there were a couple of lime-bushes growing nearby, so that you could reach out from where you sat and pick one fresh to cut with a penknife and squeeze into your tea.

What stayed clearly in my mind afterwards was the view back down-river from where we sat eating on the bank beside clear rippling shallows. Children played, Malay women in colourful sarongs moved back and forth with piles of washing on their heads, and the placid grey prehistoric-looking water buffalo munched overhanging foliage where they stood tethered in the stream. Two little boys suddenly swirled past, navigating a bamboo raft past the boulders of the stream with untroubled dexterity. It was very much an inhabited river, pre-industrial, innocent of landscaping or gentrification, an intimate part of daily life, like something from Constable's nineteenth-century Suffolk or Bewick's eighteenth-century Northumberland transposed into a climate of perpetual summer: the Stour or the upper Tyne transformed into the Ulu Penyu.

Everyone felt at home at Pasir Raja; there seems to be something universal about rivers. Desmond thought it looked like the Wye Valley. Denis thought it looked like one of the New South Wales rivers. Transported back in time, I thought about the intense rural life of Constable's paintings and Bewick's wood-engravings and John Clare's *Shepherd's Calendar*.

John Vrachnas was looking thoughtful. 'This is the sort of thing I came here for,' he said, the cynical note for once absent from his voice. 'If they'd only managed to put on something like this a couple of months ago, when we first arrived, I wouldn't have started to loathe the place so much.'

On the way back downstream there was music, but this time not from the portable radio. Kim Teng and a Chinese girl from Kuala Trengganu called Loi Joke Jong sang, Denis and Navam strummed guitars, I played the flute. We sang whatever we all knew: Carole King ('You've got a friend'); 'Yesterday'; 'Streets of London'; 'Scarborough Fair'. The Malays talked among themselves, at peace after pausing by the riverside to perform their prayers together. I found this ritual impressive and at the same time oddly embarrassing.

The singing boat swept downstream until the Chinese and Indian and Australian and English voices faded in exhaustion and we were content to glide on and on, no longer wishing to say anything more, past boulders and trailing lianas, under the gigantic broken triumphal arches of the *neram* trees, with the wallowing water buffaloes turning to stare at us as we passed.

A week later I went back by myself almost as far as Kuala Jengai to make a drawing of the river. I started off by bicycle, left the machine chained to a post by the last wayside café along the Jerangau road and hitch-hiked, feeling self-conscious. I was beginning to realise it was high time I got myself some kind of motor transport. A taxi took me ten miles to the Kuala Jengai turn-off, and I walked on for the best part of an hour (the day had not quite hotted up to its maximum yet) through overgrown rubber plantations and outcrops of forest. Occasional motor-cyclists and their pillion passengers stared in puzzlement at this *orang gila*: madman.

Eventually a cheerful Chinese driving a pick-up laden with groceries for the store in Kuala Jengai stopped to give me a lift. I clambered up into the open back and joined the Malay boy sitting on a couple of sacks of sugar and flour, between the jingling crates of soft drink bottles. We bumped away in fine style over the increasingly unsafe-looking wooden bridge and along the unsealed laterite road.

The viewpoint I had been struck by on those two previous visits was at the top of a bare hundred-foot-high slope where a strip of hillside had been embanked to build the road along its crest. The surface of the slope was crumbling bare scree where even the tenacious tropical vegetation had not yet had time to establish itself. I clipped paper to my drawing-board, took box of pastels and atomizer spray from my bag and worked concentratedly. Pastels seem to give you the best of both worlds when you are sketching a landscape: the rich colour of a painting combined with the speed and linear energy of a drawing.

When I had finished I got up stiffly. I was pink and perspiring, and my right foot had gone to sleep. I stumbled, and the open box of pastels slipped down the slope. I scrambled and slithered down in pursuit and rescued them, narrowly avoiding being caught in a landslide in the process. In the course of the hour or so I had sat there drawing, I think only a single vehicle had passed. If you were determined to lose your footing, fall down the slope in an avalanche of loose stones and break a leg, it was not the most sensible place to choose for it. But the pastels and fixative were precious; there was nowhere nearer than Singapore or Kuala Lumpur to buy them.

I walked a couple of miles back towards Jerangau, pausing by a riverside sandbank to scrub the coloured chalk from my fingers, and eventually flagged a solitary taxi with one other passenger. On the back road to Kuala Trengganu we picked up a third passenger, a middle-aged Malay ex-schoolteacher with a couple of days' worth of grey stubble. My Malay was shaky and far from fluent. His English was so rusty as to be almost incomprehensible at times, but despite that it was much more fluent than my Malay, and he was obviously glad of the chance to speak it.

The phrase 'a man who has known better days' came into my mind as we talked. He was thoughtful and touchingly seedy, like a man struggling with the everyday responsibilities of life after the death of a competent wife. When he spoke, it was clear that he looked back to colonial days, to the fifties or the beginning of the sixties. He had many friends in England, he said, in London, in Westminster, in the New Forest. Mr Jenkins, Mr Johnson, Mr Randall. They had been District Officers, Police Commissioners.

I deciphered his slurred gobbets of speech with difficulty. He had left teaching, first to become a rubber planter, then (as far as I could understand) to sell educational equipment. We stopped on the way at a roadside shop to buy a clump of some kind of green herb. 'Good for preserving food,' said the ex-schoolmaster in didactic tones. 'For preserving food. Yes.'

He wanted to know about London. Were there any illiterate people there? He seemed reassured when I said that there were, that there was even a BBC television series especially for them. Who controlled trade in Britain, he wanted to know: was it the Chinese or the Jews or the British? I explained that the Chinese do not play the same role in British society as they do in Malaysia. In fact there are supposed to be about a hundred thousand Chinese in Britain, which sounds a lot but is a negligible proportion of the population when you come to think about it. The figure in Malaysia is more like thirty per cent, a very substantial minority.

The ex-schoolteacher talked a lot about the Malaysian Chinese. 'They are remarkable people. They start with a hawker's cart in the street. The Malays are not so good at business, but the Chinese come with experience already, experience in China. They have . . . what is the word . . . *flair*. Yes, they have flair.'

But his admiration was grudging. 'People come from Indonesia and they are surprised to see it all in the hands of the Chinese. The name, you see, *Malay*sia, and yet in the hands of the Chinese. It is the same in Thailand, all business Chinese.'

I nodded equivocally, and the ex-schoolteacher abruptly tired of the overseas Chinese as a topic. 'What do you think of Malaysia?' he asked.

'Very interesting.'

'And what do you think of the development here?'

We were driving through a large oil palm plantation, perhaps a Federal Land Development Agency resettlement scheme. Oil palms, once they reach a height of ten feet or so, have an impressive prehistoric look about them, their columnar trunks snagged and shaggy with hanging epiphytic ferns like green feathers, pillars leading inwards to a receding darkness which flickers hypnotically past a moving vehicle. On the other hand, as with Forestry Commission plantations of Corsican pines in Norfolk, there are an awful lot of them, and after a few miles you begin to feel a certain monotony.

'People think that Malaysia is all covered with jungle,' he said. 'Isn't it? Eh?'

I thought of the acres of luxury air-conditioned housing for Petronas, the national oil company, at the new town of Kerteh down the coast, and the contour-planted oil palms I had seen from the air while flying across the peninsula from Kuala Lumpur: hundreds, thousands, tens of thousands of whorled thumbprints on the stripped, sun-baked, ochre-coloured earth. Jungle in the sense of neglected overgrown rubber plantation, or *belukar*, scrub-land: yes, there was plenty of that. Jungle in the sense of tall primary untouched forest of the kind I had just been trying to capture with olive green and purple-grey pastels: there was increasingly less and less of that.

I did not know what to say to the ex-schoolteacher with his stubble and his seedy clothes and his genuine pride in his country. That I wished there was a bit less 'development' and a bit more untouched jungle? That I found the wildlife of his country more interesting than its oil-palm plantations and industrial estates and blaring neon-lit shopping centres? It sounded rather selfish.

I said in as neutral a tone of voice as I could manage: 'They say that most of the forest will be cleared by the end of the century.'

The ex-schoolteacher smiled proudly. 'Soon, soon. And now we are making our own car, Proton Saga. You know this?'

Much later I made a linocut from my river sketch. Looking up at it framed on the wall, I felt I had caught something: the bright stillness of the afternoon, the river receding into blue distances. A friend looked at it one day.

'A river?' she said. 'Oh. I didn't quite know what it was. I thought it was a road.'

It had been a valiant attempt. After she had gone I took the picture down and put it in the spare room. I looked at it sadly before I closed the door on it. Perhaps, I thought, I might just as well change the forest to look like an oil-palm plantation and draw a Proton Saga saloon on the blank white bit in the middle which I had intended to represent the Sungei Penyu, the Penyu river.

One Fruit of House

Already the year was more than three-quarters of the way through. Time plays tricks in the equatorial tropics, where beyond a certain fluctuation in rainfall (between what someone called the wet season and the wetter) there are no seasonal differences to speak of. The months seemed to drift haphazardly past in an endless summer, sometimes baking hot and sunny, sometimes unpredictably deluged with rain so that white wisps of mist floated past the hills of Bukit Bauk when you looked out of the sixth-form classroom window, and the schoolchildren came into assembly in the morning with cardigans or track-suit tops draped over their shoulders even though the temperature probably never dropped below seventy degrees Fahrenheit.

The only seasonal commentary was provided by the sea, which by October had begun to turn noticeably rougher with the first premonitions of the *landas*, the north-east monsoon season. The previous month I had walked along the beach at night with friends, hoping to catch sight of a late turtle coming ashore to lay its eggs. It was calm and still in the moonlight, with the waves coming in from the South China Sea in endless glittering folds. On the way back we picked fragments of phosphorescence off the beach where the waves had deposited them: tiny scraps of substance on your fingertip, shining blue-white in the dimness like the eye of a fish. But there were no turtles.

Now, at the end of October, when a group of us were having a farewell meal at the Kuantan Hyatt hotel above Telok Chempedak beach, the waves surged up beneath us almost to the edge of the building, their creaming foam brightly illuminated by floodlights. At Kuala Penyu too it was what the Australians thought of as surfing weather. It was a restless time. It made me feel I wanted to be away, to be on the move, to cut off the expiring term in its death-throes and have a change of scene.

The Ministry passed on its belated decision about the next year on the third of November, two weeks before we were due to break up for the long holiday. Britain was back in favour again, and the following year's intake of sixth-form students were to be prepared for GCE 'A' levels: chiefly science subjects, with an accompanying programme of English language and 'study skills' to be taught by us. The new project would need far fewer teachers. There was much talk of redeployment, which meant that some of us would have to move to schools elsewhere in the country to teach 'straight' English language to forms Four and Five. It was a major upheaval, and we were asked to state our preferences, even though there was no guarantee that we would all get them.

Jim and John, who for different reasons were both increasingly dissatisfied with life in Malaysia, announced their intention of going back to Sheffield and Melbourne respectively. Terrie and Dennis Ferman-Castles, Pam, David and Monica learned that they were to be transferred to a town on the West Coast. Denis Hewett and I were to stay in Kuala Penyu, which was what we both wanted. Desmond was to be transferred to a far corner of the country. Terrie Ferman, serious, concerned and humane as ever, discussed the delicate subject of his personal hygiene with the group.

'Listen, the guy's going to start a new job in a new town a long way away. He ought to be given the chance to make a fresh start, and when I say fresh I mean fresh. What d'you say I have a word with him?'

We agreed whole-heartedly. At last someone was volunteering to take Desmond in hand. The last time it had happened was during a week's holiday, which he had spent in Bangkok. He had come back wearing a new shirt and smelling faintly of talcum powder, though not for long. He had obviously enjoyed himself.

'They're really lovely girls. Not scrubbers at all. Really good. They give you value for money all right. Not like African girls. Do you want to know something about African girls?'

There was no clamour of interest, but he went on regardless, his gaze shifting from side to side like a radar aerial. His voice turned conspiratorial.

'They smell. They really stink.'

He mistook our amazed silence for disbelief. 'It's true. They really smell bad.'

Jim and I looked at each other, lost for words.

'Really stink, African girls.' Desmond nodded to himself in recollection as a last dissolving hint of Thai talcum powder wafted across the canteen table.

'You know what I think?' said Jim to me afterwards. 'Those Thai girls. As soon as he walked in they must have torn the clothes off his back. He probably thought they were hungry for him. They just wanted to burn them.'

'And then give him a bath.'

'That's right. In sheer self-preservation.'

'I suppose it casts a new light on the meaning of the word *scrubber*.'

After the general end-of-term dispersal we heard nothing more from, or about, Desmond. I saw Terrie and Dennis Ferman-Castles a couple of years later in Brisbane. We talked about everything under the sun, and suddenly I remembered Desmond.

'Terrie,' I said, 'I don't like to bring up subjects that are best forgotten, but . . . tell me, did you ever get round to telling Desmond . . . you know, what his best friends had never managed to?'

She looked faintly embarrassed. 'Well, quite honestly, when it came to it I just didn't have the courage. It really is a very hard thing to say to someone.'

Even that fabled Australian bluntness has its limits.

I have an informal photograph of the group which I took in the school canteen before we all dispersed. Only Pam Hagan is absent. I have no idea what was actually being said at the time, but it is not hard to reconstruct some convincing story to make sense of people's expressions. Obviously Monica is saying something obscene to Denis Hewett. Jim is convulsed with disbelieving, half-shocked laughter. Terrie cannot believe her ears. John, at the other end of the table, mutters something cynical to David Hagan. Desmond, looking blankly at a bottle of chili sauce on the table in front of him as he daydreams about his next action holiday in Bangkok or Haadyai, ignores the lot of them.

It had been nice, for a while, to be part of a large expatriate group (large by local standards, at any rate), to share jokes and gossip. A shifting group of us used to meet every Monday to watch MASH on Jim's black-and-white televison. We would take it in turns to produce a communal dish of some sort to accompany it. Aside from being funny and sometimes touching, the programme seemed to make a lot of sense to me; here was a bunch of Westerners keeping their sanity and good humour, despite considerable provocation (from within as well as without) in an Asian country. I felt the kinship.

Later, on a visit to England, I mentioned this to a friend, who looked at me as though I were mad. It seems to be a breach of etiquette, in the intellectual substratum of the Western world, to make any connection between a television programme and the world you live in. You are supposed to enjoy it mindlessly, in the manner of a habit-forming drug, or else (especially in Britain) to make cleverly snide comments about it. My attitude was all wrong. I realised that I was getting out of touch.

Monica, at least, benefited from her move away from the East Coast. Three months later Denis and I received a characteristic letter from her: 'Would you feel like spitting in the air if I told you the West Coast is INFINITELY nicer than Penyu-by-the-Pigsty? No, you wouldn't. I forgot. You love coconut trees, endless beaches with not a semi-nude female body on them, lots and lots of goats and overflowing rubbish-bins and semi-comatose Malays and those picturesque mosques burping out to the faithful. Anyway, each to his own piece of Paradise.'

I benefited too. John Vrachnas had found himself a house not very far from the school, two or three miles away from the town centre and my landlord Rasul's enclave. I saw it before he left and fell in love with it at once. It was only a hundred yards behind the beach, facing an expanse of land rather like an un-gentrified English village green or common: coarse grassland with white swathes of sand prominent, as on the very poorest kind of heathland, dotted with burnt palm-stumps and the mauve-flowering bushes called (misleadingly) Singapore rhododendrons. Around this open expanse were groves of coconut palms whose fallen fronds were regularly burned in the rubbish-pits which the people of the surrounding kampong had dug at intervals in the almost pure sand of the soil. Other Malay houses were scattered round about, largely hidden by coconut palms, mango and jackfruit and cashew and sea-apple trees.

This stretch of coast was known as Sura Jetty, and a line of rotting wooden posts still marched thirty yards out to sea from the adjacent beach. These were all that remained of the jetty where a long-vanished railway line had brought iron ore from Bukit Besi inland to be loaded on to cargo ships.

Even in the deluges of the north-east monsoon season which had just begun in earnest (it was half-way through November), soaking me as I cycled back and forth running my errands, 59A Jalan Kenanga looked an enchanting house. In estate agent's language it was a bijou residence, which is to say that a family with children would have found it cramped but it was ideal for a single man. It was painted amber and cream, beautifully set in the dappled shade of the coconut palms, far lighter and brighter and airier than ecclesiastical 4F Jalan Nibong. At night the sound of the surf was clearly audible. Apart from this it was blessedly quiet. The nearest thing to a disturbance was the sound of the kampong children playing happily on what I thought of as the common, but I enjoyed that.

True, there was no fenced compound, and the indoor loo appeared to have been made for a contortionist dwarf rather than a five-foot-ten European, but these were trivial complaints. The only thing which caused me a few moments of unease was that the water came not from a mains supply but from a well behind the house. An electric pump raised water from this to fill a tank on stilts. I was safe from interruptions in the public water supply, which happened quite often, but I had my doubts about the pump. In the event it was the only thing about the house which ever gave me any trouble.

The kampong round about was solidly Malay. My landlady's name was Wan, which is one of those odd Malay honorifics – there are different ones in different parts of the country – which indicate some sort of ancient aristocratic connection but are so widely inherited they no longer have any aristocratic overtones. It was rather like Hardy's Durbeyfields who had once been D'Urbervilles. She was a thin, rather serious and preoccupied woman in her late thirties. The preoccupation was understandable because her husband had died only a month before, aged no more than forty. She was philosophical about it in that placid, quietly-spoken Malay way which leaves you unable to guess at the depth, or otherwise, of someone's feeling.

'*Dia meninggal*,' she said simply: he passed away.

There were four children. Yuri was a skinny, foolish, amiable young man, happy when he was repairing either his small motorbike or the malfunctioning pump above my well. Zam, the twenty-year-old daughter, was stunningly beautiful, the family skinniness modified in her into slender grace. There were two younger boys, Din and Sukirman. We had fractured conversations which enlarged my vocabulary with frustrating slowness. I would guess at words and surreptitiously check them in my dictionary afterwards. There was something satisfying about having guessed right; the teacher of English abroad who is totally hopeless at picking up other languages himself cuts a faintly ridiculous figure.

My Malay never became fluent (partly because in Malaysia, even on the East Coast, you can conduct so much of your life in English), but at least it improved. Wan would point to the standpipe outside my house and say what my mind registered as: 'Can I *pinjam* your water?' It was a fair assumption that *pinjam* meant 'borrow', which I was pleased to find it did when I checked. Sukirman the youngest child, who was five or six, would wander inquisitively into the house from time to time. 'Sukirman isn't *kacau*-ing you?' Wan would ask – or at least my mind would understand it as that – and the word 'disturb' would flash in my mind. Back to the dictionary: right again. But I would still kick myself for my laziness, for learning so slowly, for needing to have simple things repeated before my ears could register them.

Malay (or Indonesian, which bears about the same relationship to it as American to British English, or Argentine to Castilian Spanish) is often said to be an exceptionally easy language to learn. This comment, however, is invariably made by people who have only mastered the basics of it themselves and whose authority is therefore questionable. It is rather as though someone who had got as far as changing a spark-plug were to tell you that motorcycle repairs are exceptionally straightforward.

The truth as far as I was concerned was more restricted. It is a pretty straightforward business to pick up enough simple *Melayu pasar* or *Melayu kampong* – 'market' or 'village' Malay – to enable you to exchange greetings or buy vegetables. The grammar is easy enough, compared to a European language. There is no verb which corresponds to our 'to be', so that you can simply say 'I teacher'; 'this my friend'. There is none of that intricate structure of gender and agreement which makes German, say, or modern Greek, so full of pitfalls. To all intents and purposes there is no article at all, hence no juggling with *le* and *la* and *der* and *die* and *das* and *dessen* and *deren* and all the other confusing European variations.

Nor, most importantly, is there any equivalent of the structure of tenses which all European languages (as far as I know) cling to, as though the single most important consideration when speaking or writing were to establish a complex mathematical grid showing what order everything has happened in, or had happened in, or is happening in, or might be on the point of having been about to have just started happening in. From an Asian point of view all this manipulation of verbs must seem bizarrely unnecessary. Malay verbs are not required to perform a repertoire of contortions. Instead the language uses sensible straightforward 'marker' words like *sudah* which has the force of 'already' and hence makes the equivalent of a perfect or past tense. *Saya sudah makan:* 'I already eat', in other words 'I've eaten'. Then there is *belum* which has the force of 'not yet', and *akan* which gives a future meaning. Or there is *nanti* which literally means 'wait' and corresponds fairly closely to 'by-and-by': *saya datang nanti malam* would mean literally: 'I come by-and-by night-time', in other words 'I'll come tonight' or 'I'm coming tonight'.

So far, so straightforward. Already you find yourself wondering why the European Economic Community, with its absurd budget for translation and interpretation (forty per cent of the overall figure according to some reports, which one hopes are wildly exaggerated) does not shift to the use of Malay – either Malaysian or Indonesian – for all its official business. But then the complications, ignored by those who say 'Oh, Malay's such a *simple* language,' start to make themselves felt. The structure is straightforward enough, but structure is only one aspect of a language. Malay, if you like, resembles a car whose chassis and moving parts are very simple, but whose controls are subtle and complicated.

Shorn of its contemporary coinages, the original language grew out of a hierarchical society in which the positions of sultan and commoner were sharply defined. It is also based on the assumption that all those who speak it, as in a village where everybody knows everybody else, stand in some recognisable equivalent of a family relationship to each other: any older woman is *makcik*, 'auntie', any older man is *pakcik*, 'uncle', any woman of around your own age is *kakak* – 'elder sister' – any child is *adik*, 'younger sibling'. It does not readily adapt to use as a neutral means of communication between democratic equals.

Try to talk to other people about yourself, and even if the grammar is straightforward and the basic vocabulary fairly easily learned, the problems soon become apparent. If you refer to yourself you are *saya* which is polite or *aku* which is either colloquial or intimate. If you are writing about yourself in a narrative you are *teman*. And the simple English word 'you' is almost untranslatable; it could be *awak* or *kamu* or *kau* or *engkau*. Or it could be *anda*, which is a modern 'democratic' coinage; you see it written but no-one (confusingly) would ever dream of saying it to anyone else. Or it could be *tuan* ('Sir') or *encik* ('Mister') or *puan* ('Madam'), or simply the person's name. Wan never used a word for 'you' when she talked to me; I was always 'Peter', as though she were asking about someone else, a friend of mine perhaps, who was not there.

If you find yourself talking to a Sultan you must use different words. Husbands and wives have different modes of address again. Many Malaysians use the English word 'you' when speaking Malay, which sounds odd to an English-speaker but saves a lot of trouble. In some urban Malay dialects people use Hokkien Chinese *lu* for 'you' and *gua* for 'I'. Indonesians may use *saudara* for 'you', which is a polite way of saying 'my friend'. Bruneians have their own coinage, *awda* which is short for *Awang-Dayang*, 'Mr-Mrs', hence 'you (polite) of whichever sex.'

Things, in other words, are not so straightforward as they seem at first. If the EEC were to take up my recommendation and adopt Malay for its official dealings, a devoutly Roman Catholic MEP from Spain might greet the Pope as *Tuan* in place of 'you' or 'usted', but Mr Paisley would probably use *kau* which makes a better vehicle for deliberate rudeness. *Kau babi!* a girl might snap out at a boy pestering her. It means 'you pig!' and for obvious reasons sounds more insulting to a Muslim than it would to a bacon-and-egg-eating Briton.

I had some encouragement in my attempts to improve my Malay once I was established in the Sura Jetty house. Two tiny sisters from one of the kampong houses towards the beach, not more than three or four years old, used to look in through the wooden railings as I sat reading on the veranda. They would smile dazzling gap-toothed smiles, giggle, pick up various small objects lying around on the white sand and reluctant grass of the village 'common' and wave them at me.

'*Ini apa?*' What's this?'

'*Itu kayu*,' I would say. '*Itu bungkus.*'

'*Cakap puteh kali*,' they would shout, giggling: 'say it in white-language.' So I would say it in English: 'It's wood. It's a packet.' And they would run away, laughing merrily at this strange foreign clown.

If my Malay was making slow headway, at least I was getting fluent in Malaysian English, which was very much part of local life. At one level it is a kind of pidgin based on Malay or Chinese syntax: the shopkeeper saying 'Aw-reddy fi-nish' when something is out of stock, the monosyllabic 'can' to mean anything from 'yes, I can' to 'of course that would be all right'. But even the English spoken by fluent speakers has its own flavour. 'Get in,' says a friend opening the door of his car, 'and I will send you to the hotel.' You imagine yourself being passed on like a package until you realise he is offering you a lift. Someone else says, 'Can I follow you?' meaning not 'can I start a little way behind you, because I don't know the way' but 'can I come with you?'

Often you are asked where you stay, but the word has no 'temporary' overtones, it means (in our terms) 'where do you live?' Malaysians do not move house, they shift. 'Slang' means what we would call 'accent'; Benny Kim said to me in Kuantan: 'Mungo has kept his Scottish slang.' If a Malaysian says he 'slept late', he does not mean he stayed in bed until eleven in the morning, he means he went to bed late the night before.

The variation which I found most bizarre was the business of 'enumerators', because it showed how you can glimpse ghosts of other languages looming behind English in countries which acquired it comparatively late in their history. The only example I can think of in Standard English is the slightly old-fashioned use of the word 'head' to count cows, as in 'two hundred head of cattle'. Perhaps 'pair', as in 'a pair of trousers', or 'piece', as in 'a three-piece suit', are the same kind of thing. I am not enough of a linguist to be able to say. Other than these isolated examples, at any rate, English (like other European languages) seems to get by without feeling the need for words like this, just as Asian languages get by without our paraphernalia of tenses. But Malay, like Chinese and Japanese (none of which are related to each other, any more than any of them is to English), finds it all-but-impossible to count things or people without these enumerators or 'counting words'.

Thus, if you want to buy limes in the market you would not say simply *enam limau nipis*, six limes, but *enam biji limau nipis*, literally 'six seeds of lime'. Any other small solid things which can be held in the hand are also counted using *biji*. For thin hard things you would use the word *keping*, so that if you ask for two enlargements of a negative at the photographer's you are literally asking for two slices of photograph. Big things – houses, countries – are counted using *buah* which literally means 'fruit': *sepuluh buah rumah teres*, ten fruits of terraced house. *Batang* – stick – is used for narrow, generally stick-shaped things like trees or cigarettes. *Tiga batang kelapa* would be 'three sticks of coconut', in other words three coconut trees, whereas *tiga biji kelapa* – 'three seeds of coconut' – would be three coconuts. Human beings are counted using *orang*: *lima orang guru*, five persons of teacher, i.e. five teachers.

There are various other enumerators. Working out the correct one to use can make a complicated and absorbing game for the learner of Malay. Apples? Use *biji*. Cars? Use *buah*. Children? Use *orang*. But how do you count dreams, or molecules, or stars, or heartbeats, or dead bodies, or unsuccessful attempts?

The habit of using enumerator-words, what the linguists call 'numerical coefficients', is something very deeply-rooted in these Asian languages, so that many Malaysians and Singaporeans find it impossible to believe there is no equivalent system in English and proceed to invent one. I once went into a mini-market in Singapore to buy a lemon.

'One,' I said, pointing.

The fruit-seller looked at me blankly. He spoke English, but he could make no sense of the naked number.

'One piece,' he asked, 'or one dollar?'

'One piece,' I said, guessing what he meant. I got my lemon, and it was a whole one.

I once got entangled in confusion at a cake-shop which displayed a fine range of individual cakes as well as slices of a large one. In the kind of English I am used to there is a clear distinction between a cake and a piece of cake, but not in English-speaking South-East Asia where all kinds of objects find themselves being counted in 'pieces' (or sometimes in 'units') for lack of any other English alternative.

'Two cakes,' I said.

The Chinese girl took her tongs and picked out two slices of cream cake. 'This one-aa?'

'No, not pieces. Two *cakes*.'

But communication had broken down altogether. There seemed to be no way I could make the distinction. In the end I took the tongs and picked out the cakes I wanted myself.

Newspaper advertisements talked about new housing developments: '22 UNITS OF TERRACED HOUSES'. My current receipt from the picture-framers in Bandar Seri Begawan shows that I have had not '2' pictures but '2 nos.' of pictures framed. An otherwise perfectly literate article in the New Straits Times, describing a Malaysian painter's exhibition in Kuala Lumpur, said that the painter was showing 'twenty-five pieces of her paintings', which made it sound as though a jealous rival had got in early with a sharp pair of scissors.

My favourite example was on a competition notice I saw pinned up in Kota Kinabalu, in Sabah:

FREE
One piece of key chain
FOR
every 5 packets of Lucky Strike Filter 20 sticks.

The fourth of January was the anniversary of my arrival in Malaysia. I had slept for twelve hours the night before as a delayed after-effect of the journey back from my holiday. 59A Jalan Kenanga, Sura Jetty, was peaceful and welcoming, the kind of house which tempts you to stay up, however tired you may be, smoking one more pipe and listening to one more cassette.

When I switched the music off it was after midnight. I could hear the crashing of the monsoon-season surf, muffled by the screening coconut palms. A small herd of red-brown cattle (so many head in English, so many tails – *ekor* – in Malay) was grazing outside on the sandy common. The moon was nearly full. I had another year of my contract in Trengganu ahead of me. Despite everything, it seemed a good place to be.

SURA BEACH, MIDNIGHT

The moon has spun a patient web of cloud
Around herself, to catch stars
In the interstices.

Dry lightning flashes
At the edges of the sky, and foam
Skitters along the shore like a fuse
That has caught fire.

But there is no thunder, no explosion:
Only the patient sea repeating
Certain ancient and endless syllables
Too slowly for me to catch.

I scrunch back across the sand,
My patience no match for theirs.

PART FOUR

A Spin with Mr Tan

It may seem inconceivable that anyone could reach his late thirties in the industrialised Western world without holding a driving licence. In fact if you grow up with a reasonably efficient system of public transport and take the odd twenty-minute walk in your stride (or your saunter), it is natural enough. Confronted by the traffic in nineteen-eighties London, in fact, you sometimes wonder why anyone ever gets as far as bothering to learn.

Coaches and share-taxis meant that long-distance travelling between Malaysian towns was cheap and easy, if sometimes hair-raising. The problem was local transport. In the new house I was near the school but at least three miles from the town centre. For a time, back at 4F Jalan Nibong, Jim and I had used the rattletrap maroon-and-grey buses of the Thong Aik company which trundled between Kuala Penyu and the next town to the south. Their route took them conveniently past the school gates, though their timing was (to put it charitably) flexible.

There were some things to be said in favour of the Thong Aik buses. The muscular control you were forced to learn as you struggled not to collapse into a heap of construction workers every time the bus stopped undoubtedly helped to develop muscle tone where there had been no muscle tone before. As for the jolting, it may well have had a tonic effect on the liver. Even so, it seemed to me after a couple of months that something more enterprising was called for. I weighed up the various possibilities.

Transport can be a problem in the developing world. There is generally a *bas* (in Malaysia), or a *bis* (in Indonesia), or a minibus or a Colt or a *bemo* or an *oplet* or a *colectivo*, but you soon find that a proper British enthusiasm for buses and trains (as with the queues which accompany them) is not understood. Everywhere in those parts of the developing world where an affluent middle class has recently separated from the rest of the population, public transport has all the social acceptability of halitosis. It is this which condemns the efforts of well-meaning environmentalists and intermediate technologists to futility. Only the poor travel by bus, so that the possession of a car is the all-important symbol of status.

As for a motor-bike, it is not even seen as vaguely raffish. It is just a badge of youth and relative poverty. But at least it is better than a bicycle, which spells social disaster. Nothing in my own rather mixed-up life had prepared me for the developing world's obsession with social conformity. Every grade of affluence has its prescribed symbols, from the businessman's Mercedes and Italian leather furniture down to the labourer's bicycle.

All this is familiar enough in the West, of course. But there are two significant differences from a country with a long-established middle class like Britain: nobody blurs the categories by making an off-beat personal selection from the available range of consumer goodies, and nobody is ever so nonconformist or irreverent as to poke fun at the whole business of conspicuous consumerism. Status is taken very seriously. There are no absent-minded academics with leather elbow-patches on their jackets, no Guardian readers driving Renault 4s. And a university student in Malaysia would as soon appear in his underpants in public as be seen riding a bicycle to the lecture-hall.

I once told a story to a group of Malaysian colleagues which involved a managing director arriving for a meeting in the City of London on a number 11 bus. I was met with blank disbelief.

'A *managing director*? On a *bus*?'

Not for the first time it was the Occidentals who came across as inscrutable, perverse, the followers of bizarre customs. In many ways the strangest aspect of life in the East was its straightforwardness. Affluence, respectability, poverty: all these were as clearly delineated as separate countries on a coloured political map. It came out, for example, in people's attitude to clothes. We Westerners tend to pride ourselves on not judging people by the way they dress, because we have found out by experience how misleading this can be in a nonconformist society. Asians on the other hand (as can be seen from their unmitigated hatred and loathing of 'hippies') expect to judge people by their clothes, because in a more cohesive and traditional society appearance is a fairly reliable guide. Whether you are a beggar or a business executive you are expected to look the part.

Wanting to look like a democratic, unpretentious, classless citizen, just dishevelled enough at the edges for nobody to accuse you of being a snob, is a Western – perhaps especially a British – inhibition.

It all went together with the literal-mindedness, the lack of irony or cynicism, the unquestioned respect for authority. It was refreshing, especially after the sneering self-entanglement of British society, but it also caused odd stirrings of rebellion in the resident Westerner. Finding yourself in a world where Authority was always obeyed, not always enthusiastically but without any serious questioning, you felt the lure of childish naughtiness. I once managed to get a bet going near the beginning of school assembly on how long the headmaster would speak for. Denis Hewett, Navam, Kim Teng, Faroushee and I each put in a dollar, nearest guess to scoop the pool. Looking back it seems silly enough, but it helped to enliven the proceedings.

Kim Teng won the five dollars with the lowest guess: twenty minutes. She knew the form; he was due to present the sports awards afterwards, and hence did not have the time to give a record-breaking solo performance.

The time had come to move one step up the transport ladder. I had learned to drive a car after a fashion, though never so as to convince a British driving instructor of the fact. At the age of nineteen I had briefly steered a Lambretta around the country lanes of East Suffolk. My chief memory was a painful one of skidding on a patch of black ice into a ditch. It was not a promising background. All the same, when I heard that Mr Loo the grocer had a small motor-bike for sale I took a deep breath and cycled into town to have a look at it.

The heart of Kuala Penyu, by the estuary, was a crossroads lined with Chinese shops. Down the side-axis, Jalan Lim Teck Wan, was a stretch of pavement where pungent-smelling sharks'-fins, the severed bones protruding like teeth in a jawbone, were laid out to dry. Beyond this was a small Chinese bakery which turned out quite palatable white bread. It was one of the few bakeries in the country which did not put either sugar or yellow dye in its loaves. In a dark inner cavern like an alchemist's kitchen a smiling boy would hand you a fresh crisp loaf, blinking in puzzlement as you explained with much gesturing that you did not want it put in the slicer and nor (unlike all local customers) did you want the dark crust scraped off.

Loo's grocery, or mini-market, was on the corner of that central cross-roads. From a European point of view it was far and away the best source of groceries for miles around, better even than anything in Kuala Trengganu. There were not many other foreigners in Kuala Penyu itself, but thirty miles or so to the south was a new township which had grown up around the needs of the offshore oil installations. There was also an enormous power station under construction not far north of this which involved a French contractor, and an encampment of air-conditioned Portakabins built by Caltex, so that there were a fair number of Westerners a little way down the coast, together with communities of Japanese and Koreans. Mr Loo was the only local tradesman who had fully woken up to the fact that both Westerners and North-East Asians would pay through the nose for supplies of their own peculiar foodstuffs, from Southern Comfort or Swiss cheese to pickled seaweed.

He was a trim poised elderly man who operated his electronic till with the trace of a smile. The smile seemed to be directed inwards, rather than to the customer. He had good reason for it, especially on Thursday evenings when Toyota Land Cruisers full of Caltex housewives would descend on his shop with cries of glee and shopping baskets capacious as sacks.

His son, Young Loo, was plump and jolly, with a lank black hairpiece which was so ill-fitting that it drew attention to itself every time you looked at him. Smiling more effusively than his father, he would complain as he counted limes or weighed cheese about the discriminatory policies of the government, how inefficient feckless Malays were always given preference over frugal, competent, hard-working Chinese. Any mention of Singapore – the nearest thing to a working model of Malaysia with the Chinese in charge – would unite both Loos in a moment of reverent silence. A faraway look would come into Old Loo's eyes. Young Loo, his hairpiece slipping towards one ear, would sigh gustily.

'Singapore, that Lee Kuan Yew, so clever one. So organised, business work well. Here no future. We make, they spend, these Malays.'

But the electronic till kept beeping and cheeping, and still the Texans staggered out every Thursday evening under their crates full of Southern Comfort. Old Loo smiled faintly as his son grumbled.

There was an Even Younger Loo whom I never met who was studying in Kuala Lumpur, and it was this younger son who was disposing of his motor-bike. Old Loo took me across the road to the garage near the Kasanya Hotel where this was being kept. It was a blue Yamaha 80 cc step-through, hardly the stuff of which macho dreams are made, but the right kind of thing to start on. We haggled briefly and I paid the exorbitant price being demanded. 'I will include the transfer fee,' said Loo magnanimously, a sure sign that he was making a killing and knew it. He smiled faintly as I wheeled the machine away into a back street to wrestle with the intricacies of its clutchless gears.

Most vehicles have their teething troubles. Even Younger Loo's motorbike had not so much teeth as fangs, tusks, tombstones. On that first day I contented myself with riding it slowly and rather insecurely home. The following day I took it on to the quiet sea-front road again and rode in the opposite direction, away from the town towards the hills of Bukit Bauk as far as the Golf Club. At this slightly run-down establishment, whose dilapidated rattan furniture still retained a seedy remnant of elegance, I stopped for coffee, looking out over the grey windswept monsoon-season sea, then set off the three miles back home. I was moving out from a lane entrance into the main road when the throttle suddenly roared of its own accord up to full, throwing me on to the side of the road.

I remounted and limped on as best I could, controlling the machine with the footbrake, as far as a workshop a little way along the main road run by a couple of young Chinese.

The throttle cable was duly repaired. Later in that first week the indicators failed and the battery ran out. I began to feel nostalgic for my bicycle, which I had left unchained in the town centre in the excitement of collecting the Yamaha. By the following day, when I remembered, it had vanished. But the teething troubles were sorted out one by one at the workshop, where the two young Chinese gave me pitying glances each time I wheeled the machine in. Throttle-cable . . . carburettor . . . piston-head . . . I began to understand what slow learners at school must go through: the blurred ungraspable concepts, like out-of-focus diagrams on an overhead projector, the booming incomprehensible monologues of the teacher, the looks of pitying disbelief from the brighter children.

It was like being back at school studying 'O' level mathematics. I blushed at my own ignorance and paid without complaining.

Reluctantly, being totally without confidence where any kind of machinery was involved, I put my name down for driving lessons at the Wong *Sekolah Memandu* or Driving School, one of a small row of down-market shophouses beside a rutted lay-by in the High Street. Next to it was a photographer's where I went to get passport-sized prints for my provisional licence. The interior of the studio was dominated by a huge wall-poster representing the faceted peaks, blue sky and tall conifers of a Rocky Mountain landscape. Standing in front of this in the full blast of the air-conditioner I felt faintly disoriented after the acacias, yellow flame trees and sweaty humidity of the street outside.

Mr Loo the grocer, despite his smiling inflexibility over prices, had a certain gentlemanly restraint and neatness about him, like the kind of Conservative politician in England who keeps his rapacity well hidden. Mr Wong was the other kind of Chinese tradesman, the kind with no leanings towards middle-class respectability. He favoured a white singlet and tatty shorts and waddled noisily across the floor on rubber flip-flops. He undertook to supervise my progress on the motorbike himself but delegated Tan Lee Ngee, a brisk handsome youngish man who I think was one of his sons-in-law, to brush up my car driving.

The Wong Driving School had a motorbike of its own, a Honda 50 with some sort of hobble on the engine to reduce its already limited power. As a result I had an endless problem distinguishing one gear from another, since the difference was only between next-to-no-acceleration (first gear) and hardly-any-acceleration (top gear). On this spindly machine I would glide up and down the High Street dodging goats, schoolchildren and bicycle-rickshaws, accompanied by an almost inaudible farting noise.

Mr Wong spoke no English, which made for complications. The Malaysian motorbike test involves a zoom-past culminating in an emergency stop, and I would practise this with Mr Wong standing massively, clip-board under his arm, plump stomach thrusting out of his white singlet, outside the gate of the tennis club. Down would come his bare arm as I passed, and I would slam hand and foot on the brakes. *'Jangan jatoh!'* Mr Wong would shout in energetic warning, making stabbing gestures with his hand towards my foot.

My self-esteem, already reduced by my humiliation over the internal combustion engine, was further eroded by this inability to understand the instructions I was being given. The old-fashioned breed of travelling Englishman looked down on foreigners who were unable to understand English, and shouted more loudly at them as his only gesture towards better communication. I was the newer breed. I felt guilty at not having mastered the language of the country after a whole year and could not help seeing myself as Wong and Tan must have seen me, as a blank-faced halfwit gobbling and mouthing at the simplest instruction. I also tended to stammer at moments of stress.

'*Apa maknanya j-j-j-jatoh?*'

But Mr Wong was quite unable to tell me what *jatoh* meant in English. In fact (I found out later) he was telling me not to land on my right foot when bringing the bike to a standstill, since that was the one which had to stay on the footbrake.

Even when it came to my car-driving lessons with Tan Lee Ngee there were occasional language problems. Driving the red Mini along the narrow beach road with the speedometer nudging thirty miles an hour I sensed Tan becoming restless. 'Oil!' he snapped out sharply. 'Oil! Oil!'

At first I was nonplussed by this. I was aware that the manufacturers had fitted a dashboard warning light, but it was not registering anything worrying.

'Oil, Mr Tan?'

He made stabbing gestures towards my feet, the kind favoured by his father-in-law. Belatedly I realised that he was telling me to put my foot down, to give it more speed. Petrol in Malay is *minyak tanah* – 'earth-oil' – generally referred to as *minyak*, 'oil' for short. We were both victims of literal translation, rather like an American driver in Britain asking for gas and being given a large blue Shellane cylinder.

Tan was horrified by my driving style. Learning in England, I had been taught to spin the wheel by slipping it between my hands, never crossing them or losing contact with the wheel for a second. 'No! No! Very bad!' shouted Tan when he saw my careful English technique. 'Cannot!'

'But that's the way –'

'No! Cannot! Must cross hand. We practise.'

And so for several afternoons, on a patch of scrub-land

rather like an overgrown bomb-site, I was set to unlearn. An observer would have seen a mildly dilapidated Mini lurching and juddering clockwise, then anti-clockwise, as though its driver were being attacked by a swarm of hornets. Furiously I spun the wheel from side to side as the car swerved round one clump of bushes after another. It was like doing chest expansion exercises.

'Cross hand!' shouted Tan, his face relentless. 'Left! Again! Faster!'

Red-faced, giddy, my back glued to the seat with sweat, I spun on, feeling like an astronaut undergoing some sort of training in high-g manoeuvring. But it was effective. Never since then have I managed to slip the wheel of a car between my hands.

Every lesson followed exactly the same pattern. This consisted of a couple of unvarying circuits of the test course: round the town centre, then a hill-start on the one small back-lane slope which rose more than a few feet above beach-level, then half an hour at the tennis club (which doubled as the Test centre) practising parking. During this second phase of the afternoon Mr Tan would stop for a cigarette and a chat with his cronies on the veranda of the club while I reversed again and again, perspiring freely, between a series of black-and-white posts. Apart from the business of learning to spin the steering wheel with my hands crossed there was never any variation in this, and after a month or so I realised that I had learned an important lesson about teaching in East Asia. For once I was on the receiving side of it, and it was illuminating.

I remembered the frequent puzzlement local teachers as well as students showed at Western teaching assumptions. What I was doing now was what they were used to. The test itself followed an identical pattern each time. No examiner would ever break the unwritten rules to the extent of getting the candidate to park in a different place, or vary the test route so as to take in a different back lane. Even if there had been a second hill in the town centre it would never have been used for the hill-start.

Tan had thought me half-witted early on when I had merely driven straight on, waiting for him to tell me whether to turn or not.

'Aiyah! Why you don't turn already?'

'But you didn't tell me —'

'No, no, must always turn here, Jalan Kambing. Got to know test route. We go back, do that again.'

The test, in other words, was something you learned by heart. When your turn came you reproduced exactly what you had learned. The examiner could sit beside you the whole way without needing to open his mouth except when he warned you that the emergency stop was imminent. You were shown something, you repeated it over and over again until you knew it by heart; finally you gave, as nearly as possible, a perfect reproduction of what your instructor had first shown you. You were then given marks according to how accurately you had managed this. It was what people expected.

As a result I still find it fiendishly difficult to park a car smoothly. But should I ever find myself back outside the tennis club at Kuala Penyu, Trengganu, I would be able to manoeuvre between the black-and-white posts with my eyes closed. I was not taught to drive, in other words, but to pass the Malaysian driving test. In the same way, nobody at school supposed that we were teaching the children to speak English. We were teaching them to pass the TOEFL examination and later the triple-one-nine (the Malaysian equivalent of 'O' level), which was not necessarily the same thing at all. It was a salutary lesson to have learned.

There were two stages to the driving test. The first was a written examination taken early on in the proceedings, when you applied for your provisional licence. It followed the multiple choice format. The questions were on the lines of *What do you do when a large lorry suddenly stops in front of you? a) go faster; b) turn left; c) turn right; d) stop.* Several candidates failed this and were led out of the room by relatives, looking shaken.

On the day originally booked for the main test I had to

begin by negotiating a bureaucratic labyrinth. When I turned up at the driving school early in the morning, Tan checked my provisional licence. Buried in the long line of numbers machine-stamped on the back, it turned out, was an expired date.

There was consternation. Wong and Tan shouted at each other in Chinese.

I was long since past showing visible distress. 'What do I do?' I asked wearily

'You must go into Kuala Trengganu, to JPJ. Take a taxi. Be back later in the morning.'

My heart sank. An hour by taxi each way, with an unspecified interlude sandwiched in the middle to be spent hanging round the JPJ, the Road Transport Office, followed by a double driving test: it was more than I could face. In the end we agreed to postpone the test for a day. Denis Hewett, who had by now moved into the house next door, was going into Kuala Trengganu that afternoon to meet his visiting parents at the airport, so we shared a taxi at leisure.

It poured with rain most of the following day, although at least this had the benefit of keeping the temperature down. There were fifty or so candidates altogether, and at eight o'clock in the morning we were all jockeying for space in the shelter of the tennis club veranda amid a pungent smell of urinals and clove cigarettes. It was a leisurely, nerve-racking process. First came the parking test in the car. There was room for two of us to do this at a time, which meant three-quarters of an hour reading discarded copies of the Star and the Malay Mail and apprehensively watching other candidates creeping round corners in reverse gear. Then came the figure-of-eight round a couple of posts on the motorbike, with an interested and critical audience. This was only the beginning.

The morning crept on. The rain stopped briefly, then started again with renewed determination. The urinal-smell grew stronger, and I was reduced to reading the classified advertisments in the Malay Mail. Finally, at a quarter to two, I took to the road for the main part of the test. It was the

first manoeuvre of the day to be performed without a large audience. Half-asleep (on a sunny afternoon I would have been unconscious by now) and faint with hunger, I stalled the car on the hill-start for the first time in years.

There was more hanging about even after this, because the motorcycle candidates still had to manage their drive-past. When my turn came I waved my arms in the appropriate signals and landed correctly on my left foot after the emergency stop. After a brief post-mortem with Tan I bought some takeaway food in the town and buzzed back to Sura Jetty on my own machine, dripping wet and in a state of total exhaustion.

Three weeks later I learned that I had passed both tests. Either the examiner had recognised the botched hill-start as a momentary lapse, or else the money I had paid Mr Wong for the course of lessons had oiled something more than the gearbox of that elderly Mini. I never made any attempt to find out.

Bread Pudding and Swiss Cheese

Now that I was mobile, the dimensions of the world around me changed. What had seemed like a major expedition on the bicycle became a short spin down the road. There were quiet kampong lanes to ride through in the late afternoon, scattering chickens and gleaning radiant smiles from children, and the inland road to Jerangau to explore at leisure.

There was something pleasantly anonymous about riding this sturdy though hardly glamorous machine. An underpowered two-wheeler might have been beneath the dignity of Malaysian teachers, but it was standard for much of the rest of the population, especially Malay teenagers whose little Yamahas and Suzukis and Honda Fames littered the streets and wove in and out of the path of timber lorries on the main road. I would sit out on my shaded veranda in the afternoon, half-dozing after school, hearing nothing more strenuous than the dry flap and rustle of coconut fronds or the merriment of the kampong children chasing one another round the common, when a thin penetrating snarl would rise above the rustic stillness. Slowly it would rise to a deafening crescendo before it abruptly faded, to be followed in quick overlapping succession by another, and another.

These were the local hell-riders, who found that the beach road, which was no use for through traffic, made a fair substitute for Bonneville Salt Flats. The little bikes would screech past at astonishing speeds with their riders stretched out prone, legs thrust out horizontally behind them. I never worked out how they managed to stop without falling off. They must have manoeuvred themselves back into a conventional posture as though on a vaulting horse.

It was because of this sort of thing, and the accident rate

which went with it, that the police mounted periodic road-blocks to check documentation and road-worthiness. Not long after buying my own machine I was caught in one of these. At the time my provisional licence had not yet come through from Kuala Trengganu. I was riding back towards the town, having been exploring the back road towards Jerangau, and by the time I saw the police car I realised there was no escape-route, no back lane I could turn swiftly into. I slowed to a reluctant halt.

'*Lesen?*' said the younger of the two policemen. At any other time he would have struck me as a smooth-faced, amiable youngster, but in these circumstances he looked forbidding. It was the classic nightmare of the essentially law-abiding person: the policemen in the Third World country with their peaked caps, the language difficulty, the non-existent documents.

I explained, stammering, that I had no *lesen*: not no lesson but no licence. Under the stress of shock I managed to string together a whole sentence as I struggled to explain that the Road Transport Department had not yet sent the licence to the driving school.

At the sound of my hesitant, inaccurate Malay he softened faintly. '*Kerja mana?*' he asked with a trace of distrust. 'Where do you work?'

'*Saya guru.* I'm a teacher.'

It was a magic word. His face softened into a smile. '*Cikgu*, eh? *Cikgu* . . . aaa . . .' He walked across to his superior and explained to him, gesturing. I tried to look as small as possible.

The sergeant walked across to me. He too was smiling. '*Cikgu*, eh?'

I could manage this level of conversation. 'Teacher, yes. At the Science School.'

They conferred again, but I could sense that the worst was past. The sergeant turned to me again. 'Next time,' he said in hesitant English, smiling more broadly, 'you . . . must have licen'. This time . . . warning only.'

I apologised profusely and rode slowly back towards the

town, knowing perfectly well that if I had turned out to be an engineer with one of the oil companies, like most of the Westerners occasionally spotted in the area, there might not have been so many smiles, perhaps even a demand for an on-the-spot fine. There were things to be said for the local attitude towards education, as I used to remind myself from time to time at school as the frustration-level rose.

The oil workers, of course, were the real expatriates. We teachers, beside them, had a peculiar ill-defined status. By local standards we were on embarrassingly high salaries. To the foreign employees of Caltex and Petronas, to the extent that they were aware of our existence, we were paupers living on barely more than a Peace Corps volunteer's pocket-money. On the whole there was no social mixing with the passengers of those Land Cruisers and shiny new company cars who came to patronise Mr Loo's grocery in the town centre.

The first contact I had was not promising. A large car stopped beside me on the road into town and an equally large Westerner with a fleshy face and cold eyes leaned out. He was wearing a cowboy hat.

'Where can Ah git some *liquor* in this town?'

His voice was drawling, but there was something almost vicious in the way he spat out the word *liquor*.

It was the middle of Ramadan, the fasting month, and even those Chinese restaurants which sold alcohol would have been careful to do so only behind closed doors. I said, 'You could get some beer at that Chinese place over there.'

The American spat in the gutter. 'Ah didn't say *beer*, Ah said *liquor*.' He directed his baleful stare at me as though he were weighing the merits of clambering out of the car and throttling me until I told him all I knew. I directed him on to Kuala Trengganu. It seemed a safe distance away.

While the Australian teachers were still in Kuala Penyu, Monica, at least, turned her sights determinedly in the direction of the Caltex camp. This was a lot more like the style to which she had become accustomed than sitting round Jim's black-and-white television on Monday evenings watching MASH over beer and fried rice.

I escorted her out to the camp one evening, where she had been invited to a barbecue. Monica circulated, assessing the marital status and economic prospects of the men. I spent most of the evening talking to a friendly middle-aged Australian couple, first about Malaysia and its complicated racial problems, then about Australia.

'They talk about Aussies being racists,' said Brian, 'but I tell you this: until I came out here to Asia to work, I didn't know what the word meant. We're a bunch of holy innocents compared to these Malaysians. They've got racism down to a fine art here. Someone scrawls a bit of graffiti on a wall in Melbourne and next day in Malaysia they're all saying how shocking it is. But have you noticed how they won't let a single Vietnamese refugee settle in this country? They park 'em on an offshore island and wait for the white countries to come and pick 'em up.'

We drove back after midnight under a yellowish moon with the lights of huge timber lorries looming up in the dark. Remembering the conversation, the food, the local touches like the small rather endearing tree-frog perched on the outside wall as we ate, I thought what an enjoyable evening it had been. Suddenly Monica's raspy voice broke into the contemplative silence.

'So Peter – you don't think I'm *too* unattractive, do you?'

I struggled out of my late-night reverie. The strange leaf-formations of the forest's edge flashed past in the headlights.

'You have a very nice figure, Monica.'

'Oh *God*, that means my face must be absolutely terrible, doesn't it?'

Reluctantly, I gave way to annoyance. 'Look, Monica, you'll have to excuse me, I have a reasonable line in relaxed small-talk, but I'm no good at manufacturing artificial compliments at half-past twelve at night.'

After this she sulked in silence for the rest of the short journey. It was one of Monica's talents that she could always make someone else feel guilty. There she was, surrounded by all these ill-mannered inconsiderate people who did not realise her central importance in the universal scheme of things. How selfish of you! You had actually sat in a car for a whole quarter of an hour prattling on about Malaysia and oil companies and food and other people and life in general and suchlike selfish trivia, without pausing to pay Monica one single reassuring compliment.

She was like a lighthouse-beacon, flashing at five-second intervals *Give me attention!* Briefly, before you blinked twice and the world settled back into normality, you found yourself apologising.

It was six months before I paid my second visit to the Caltex camp. A young English couple I had met that first evening with Monica, Roy and Julie, had invited me to a party at their house. The theme, Julie said when I met her at Loo's grocery, was to be 'VE Day'.

'Come in a bow tie if you can. Or failing that, any kind of tie will do. We're trying to do it in style.'

Julie was the sort of person for whom you would have done a great many more demanding things than putting on a tie. She was tall, slender, blonde, full of vivacious energy. I could not imagine her in repose. She was the sort of person who without necessarily having the slightest desire to lead other people would always go through life surrounded by admirers and willing assistants.

For once I was going to aim at uncompromising elegance – whether I attained it was another matter – and to hell with being a democratic, unpretentious, classless citizen. I dug out my white tropical suit and blue silk tie, not knowing what to expect.

It was an incongruous costume when riding a small motor-bike through the deepening Malaysian dusk. I had a brief glimpse of the last yellow strips of sunset inland as I zoomed across the stretch of open country outside the town, then all reminders of daylight were swallowed up in the darkness between the huge *kapor* trees of the Forest Reserve. A hail of insects spattered my face and helmet. It was about thirty-five minutes' ride to the Caltex camp, through a wooden arch by the roadside and down a bumpy track to within an Olympic stone's-throw of the beach.

The camp was a low huddle on the flat coastal strip, invisible from the main road. The houses were prefabricated, like pairs of Portakabins tacked together, but amazingly spacious inside, air-conditioned and well-furnished at company expense. Outside, they were embowered in bougainvillea. It was a little like a well-established, skilfully-landscaped mobile home site. Or at least, that was the comparison which had come into my mind on my earlier visit. This time, arriving in darkness, it was the interior luxury which impressed me.

Inside Roy and Julie's house it was not only the air-conditioning which made it feel like a different world, or at least a different continent, not to mention a different decade. A Malay girl in a tight *sarong kebaya* like the kind Malaysian or Singaporean flight stewardesses wear dispensed drinks, and when it was time for the food later a couple of male servants appeared from behind the scenes bearing dishes. Apart from this below-stairs element there was no Asian connection at all.

The guests were a representative collection of the local Anglophone expatriate community: chiefly British, but with a few Australians and a single American who seemed (understandably) a trifle bemused by the whole folk-ritual. Most worked for Caltex, a few for Petronas which is the Malaysian national oil company. A few were to do with the new power station several miles away. One was a pilot with Bristow Helicopters. Most were in their thirties or forties, a number of them much older, only a very few in their twenties. Many had worked on the Gulf, in Bahrain or Dubai, before coming on to Malaysia. Except as far as age was concerned, I was the anomaly.

Julie had done things in style. Vera Lynn was singing on cassette as I walked in. On the improvised stage someone did a Winston-impersonation ('blood . . . shweat . . . toil . . . and tearsh'), and after this a link-man took over the microphone. His commentary took the form of an apparently endless string of Irish jokes. When I set my mind to it, I can usually only remember one Irish joke. I think it must be the kind which actually originates in Ireland, because it is about a not-quite-clever-enough Englishman who is outwitted by an Irishman he wrongly assumes to be stupid. The MC's Irish jokes were the other, more familiar kind.

'Did you hear the one about the Irishman complaining about the chewing-gum machine on the wall of the loo?' The MC's parody of an Irish accent was elephantine. '"Ah, sure and begorra, you only get two for fifty pee, and dey taste of rubber."'

After five or six of these my smile was beginning to congeal. Perhaps I was turning thin-skinned. I wondered if Malays told jokes about Tamils or Sarawakians. The British were closing ranks. Only the American and I were left on the fringes of things, nonplussed anthropologists who had not done their homework thoroughly enough in the Faculty Library before going to watch the circumcision rites.

Churchill's stand-in ambled off the stage for the second time amid enthusiastic applause. 'And now,' said the MC, 'we move over to . . . THE LADIES' . . . HEALTH CLUB!' Julie and the other company wives raced on to the stage dressed in funny wigs and scarlet leotards stuffed with unlikely-looking bulges, miming a Keep-Fit class for the terminally obese.

They waddled off in mock-exhaustion, and the stage was left bare for a moment. The MC snapped into action again.

' . . . And then last of all they opened the door of the Irishman's cell and out comes Paddy. "Excuse me, sorr," he says, "but wad ye be after havin' such a t'ing as a box of matches on yez at all?"'

There were a few chuckles. A small man danced across the stage amid wild yells of delight wearing nothing but a pair of frilly knickers and waving a loo brush. Several people sang comic songs. The Bristow helicopter man forgot his words half-way through and retired sheepishly amid the loudest applause to date. The British respect a loser.

After the floor show came the food in a great array of tin trays. There was shepherd's pie, corned beef hash and potato salad, followed by bread-and-butter pudding: what a cosmopolitan English friend of mine scathingly refers to as 'nursery food'. I enjoyed it all, especially the bread-and-butter pudding. But I felt the lack of what a local feast might have had to offer: say a dish of beef *rendang*, which is a dry curry fragrant with lemon grass and coconut milk and fierce with chili, or some Malaysian-style barbecued chicken wings marinated in fresh ginger juice, turmeric and soy sauce.

But Asia had been banished to somewhere beyond the reach of the air-conditioning. We might all have been celebrating the end of ration coupons in 1951. Replete, we took the song-sheets which Julie was handing out and joined the electronic ghost of Vera Lynn in 'There'll Always Be An England'. The expatriates were re-living their Finest Hour.

It was midnight. I rode back home beneath the stars wondering whether on the evidence of that evening there was a gap at the heart of my own national culture. Why did everything have to stay at the level of knees-up burlesque? And why did the only glimmer of whole-heartedness involve something which had happened forty years before? But I also felt a twinge of guilt about what might have been my own small-mindedness. I had been invited out of pure generosity, after all, even if a detached part of my mind could not help pointing out that on Caltex salaries – at least four, perhaps five times my own – my hosts could afford it.

No. 59A Jalan Kenanga, even at night, felt steamy after the air-conditioning. It would not have met Caltex standards of executive luxury, but there was something personal as well as welcoming about the Indian rug, the Balinese carving, the Javanese *batik*-length on the wall, my own pastel landscape sketches. I took off my suit jacket and tie and relaxed with a pipe before I went to bed.

Idly I picked up the current issue of my old college's Magazine and Record, which had just been forwarded to me, and read that my friend Pete Baker was now Head of the Biotechnology Research Group at the laboratory of the Government Chemist. I looked further down the list.

It was all pretty impressive stuff. One W. R. Allen (1966) was now Director of the Thoroughbred Breeders' Association Equine Fertility Unit. R. M. C. Beak (1943) had been appointed Assistant Bishop of Mount Kenya East Diocese of the Church of the Province of Kenya . . . J. Emerson (1960) had been appointed Persian Specialist at the Widener Library, Harvard University . . . C. G. Gaggero (1949) had been appointed Knight of the Order of St Gregory the Great by his Holiness the Pope . . . Professor L. G. Jaeger (1959) had received the A. B. Sanderson Award at the Canadian Society for Civil Engineering for 'outstanding contributions to Structural Engineering' . . . M. K. Swales (1951) had led the first scientific expedition to Inaccessible Island in the Tristan da Cunha Group . . . I. R. Hobson (1970) had played Shostakovitch's Second Piano Concerto at a Promenade Concert . . . J. G. Williams (1967) had been promoted to the rank of Lieutenant-Colonel.

And meanwhile P. D. Gauld (1964) was vegetating – not too unhappily – somewhere on the eastern edge of the Malay peninsula. There was still a free Saturday ahead of me. I decided that I would take my towel across the common to the beach in the morning and practise my crawl stroke. Later perhaps Denis and I would have a game of *pétanque* on the edge of the common, where sandy tracks wound beneath the coconut palms. In the evening I would collect a takeaway *biryani* from Ismail, the gentle grey-bearded Madrasi Muslim who ran the *Muhibbah* restaurant in town and whose wooden leg creaked as he walked.

If I lived in the kampong, at least I would enjoy the kampong pleasures.

It was not only the British who sometimes ended up obsessively shutting out the Asian-ness of Asia.

One day a couple of parcels with Swiss stamps on them arrived addressed to two girls c/o Denis Hewett. One of the names was familiar to him; it was that of a girl he had met in Israel two or three years previously during his backpacking phase.

'She must be passing through here soon. That'll be interesting. Nice girl, Franziska. We were working on the same kibbutz together. She'd just been travelling round Egypt.'

I said: 'That must have been a bit of a shock for her. In my experience the Swiss tend to think the Third World starts at London. What did she make of Cairo?'

'Oh, she didn't turn a hair. She's not that sort of Swiss. She's tough.'

The parcels sat in Denis's living-room for two weeks awaiting the girls' arrival, until one day he noticed that swarms of ants were making their way into the folds of brown wrapping paper. When the parcels were opened in the interests of domestic hygiene they both proved to contain bars of Swiss chocolate, sweets and packets of cashew-nuts. The latter seemed a curious thing to send all the way from Switzerland to the East Coast of Malaysia, where cashew trees grow in abundance on the sandy soil.

Denis and I washed off the ants and put what was left of the bonbons in his fridge to await the arrival of Franziska and her friend Annette.

When they finally did arrive, their timing was unfortunate in that Denis was away in Kuala Lumpur for the weekend. The divorcés of my acquaintance were falling like timber trees in the logging concessions of Ulu Kelantan. Cyril had either just married or was on the point of marrying a Malaysian-Singhalese girl; Mungo was engaged to a Malaysian-Indian girl who was a Bahai and who also (rumour had it) was weaning him off beer. Now Denis had met a divorced Malay doctor who lived in Kuala Lumpur, and was exhausting himself travelling across the country to see her every other weekend.

Franziska and Annette arrived on a Friday evening in pitch darkness, shell-shocked after seven hours on the bus from Kuala Lumpur. They had been wandering round the town asking for directions to Denis's house, and someone had directed them to mine on the basis that one white person was pretty much like another.

They were on the homeward stretch of a round-the-world trip which had taken them at least six months so far.

'Denis . . . ?' they said hesitantly when I opened the door. I explained that Denis, who had been given no date for their arrival, was away for the weekend but that he had left his spare key at a house not very far away.

They looked blank at this. I had had nothing to eat that evening myself, and there was next to no food in the house to offer them. I suggested that they should come with me to collect the key and stop at a restaurant nearby.

They nodded, slightly unsurely, and parked their rucksacks inside my house. We walked out through the darkened, tree-hung lanes of the kampong to meet Aidah, the keeper of the spare key. She was a very slender, graceful, exotically lovely girl with a mane of black curls. She had the kind of beauty which reminded you that the Malays, in both race and language, are said to be related to the Polynesians of Samoa and Tahiti. The key was in the house which belonged to her fiancé's father, and here the three of us were inveigled into watching part of a Malay film on television, a non-stop sequence of slapstick violence.

The fiancé's father was the local bird-singing champion, so that the entire living-room was stacked with bird-singing cups and trophies which gleamed in the dim light. Malays breed several kinds of bird in the same way that the miners of North-East England breed pigeons, but among the Malays it is the song which is highly fancied. Five or six of the elegant little bell-shaped cages hung from the ceiling. Except for the television, it was like an Oriental Old Curiosity Shop.

The birds themselves, the *burong ketitir* or ground-doves, were like small slender pigeons with faint zebra stripes like unusually Quakerish budgerigars. I peered into their cages in the flickering television-lit gloom, making encouraging noises. *Thud . . . Aaaargh . . . Aiyaaah . . .* came the sound of unarmed combat. The *burong ketitir* clanked their drinking bowls gently, perhaps in disapproval, but otherwise remained disappointingly silent.

From here we walked a few yards on to a Chinese restaurant on the main road. During the period of the

Australian occupation groups of us had shared an occasional cheerful feast here. The Saujana had a few circular tables outside and several more in the small air-conditioned interior. Its speciality was seafood: prawns of all sizes, steamed fish, shellfish, cuttlefish, crab, searing hot Thai *tom yam* soup.

'What about some fried rice?' I said when they showed no enthusiasm at this list. 'Or vegetable soup? They don't only do seafood.'

Franziska and Annette protested that they had eaten some bananas and oranges on the bus and did not really want any more. 'But maybe we haf a Pepsi . . .'

Perhaps, I thought, they had upset stomachs. But I was hungry myself, and having got this far I was reluctant simply to walk back home to my own almost bare larder and make do with a cheese sandwich.

'Well, you won't mind if I have something myself? I won't be long, because I know you're probably tired.'

'No, no, not at all. Please.'

I ordered fried rice, which was particularly good at the Saujana, and a dish of sizzling beef with ginger. I noticed out of the corner of my eye that when the plate of fried rice arrived Annette pulled her chair three feet away from it. I looked enquiringly at her.

'We don't like seafood,' she said rather primly. 'You see, to us it is like eating . . .' From a safe distance she pointed at the fried rice, which was littered with prawns and sections of cuttlefish. 'What is the name . . . ?'

'Caterpillars,' said Franziska.

'Ja. Like eating caterpillars.'

I reflected that the Swiss, coming from a landlocked country, must have little experience of seafood. Probably the average Chinese, confronted for the first time with a cheese fondue, would feel equally squeamish.

It seemed a pity that I had chosen the Saujana, but after what emerged later I realised that the choice of restaurant would have been immaterial. Denis came back from his weekend of wooing in the capital, and I saw nothing more of the Swiss girls until a couple of days later, when I joined the three of them for tea at the Tanjong Jara hotel up the coast, a luxurious beach-side Malay palace of dark carved wood set incongruously in what looked like a Japanese landscaped garden.

We walked back along two miles of deserted beach, took the homeward ferry across the estuary and stopped to buy groceries at Loo's shop in the town. Franziska and Annette, who so far had struck me as a remarkably subdued pair, discovered that enterprising Mr Loo stocked Emmenthal cheese at considerably below Swiss prices. They began to show signs of animation.

When they also discovered packets of Knorr soup and Australian spaghetti and tins of Australian tomato paste they were positively excited. They left the shop with a bagful of imported groceries, and we went back to Denis's house to meet Sam, a friendly young Indian engineer from Telekoms who dropped in now and then to play a game of chess with him.

The clock ticked round to seven o'clock, and someone suggested food.

'What about fetching a couple of *murtabaks* from the Bumi?' said Denis.

Sam and I agreed whole-heartedly. The Bumi was a small Malay restaurant not far away, and a *murtabak* is a kind of pancake in several layers filled with curried meat, served with a lentil dip and a sweet-sour raw vegetable mix. At its best it is one of the most delicious (and substantial) snack meals I know, a great deal nicer than the average limp, chemically-flavoured fast-food-chain hamburger. A lot of Asian food takes some getting used to on the part of the European palate, but *murtabak* usually crosses the cultural gap quite easily. Hence it makes a good dish to try on visiting foreigners.

Sam went off on his motorbike to the restaurant while Franziska and Annette bustled into the kitchen to make Knorr soup from the packets they had bought. We all had a bowlful.

'It is good?' asked Annette, hovering over us.

Fine, we said. And now some *murtabak*?

They recoiled – there was no mistaking it – in horror. 'It's all right,' I said as reassuringly as I could, 'there's no seafood in it. No caterpillars.'

But that, it seemed, was not the point, and after a few tactfully probing questions the grisly truth emerged: they simply could not bring themselves to try any kind of Asian food whatever except bananas and oranges which of course came in their own hygienically sealed wrappings.

'And dere were *a-ni-mals* in Denis's rice when we looked in the jar,' said Annette in her Helvetic sing-song, as if that represented the final damning detail.

'Animals?' repeated Denis, puzzled, perhaps visualising mouse-deer and flying squirrels.

'A-ni-mals, ja, de small ones.'

'I think they must mean weevils,' I said.

'Well, of course there are. All rice has got weevils in it here when you buy it. They don't kill them with poisonous chemicals. It's easy enough to rinse them out.'

Franziska and Annette were both nice-looking girls, and I dare say it would never have occurred to Sam, who was only twenty-two and susceptible, to be offended by their attitude. All the same, I felt embarrassed on his behalf. In England I suppose a foreigner might just get away with a wholesale dismissal of the native food, since a fair number of English people are uncomfortably aware that their standard diet has yet to catch the attention of the world's gourmets. But in Asian countries, as in France or Italy, food is fundamental, the basis of social life and national identity as well as mere nutrition, and I would not have blamed Sam for feeling hurt.

Their UTA ticket had taken the girls across the Atlantic to the United States, where they had spent some time. From Los Angeles their route had taken them on to Tahiti (which they had loathed), New Zealand (which they had loved), New Caledonia (which they had loathed), and Australia, where they had bought a second-hand car and travelled round for a couple of months. They had spent nearly all their time in 'white' countries, in other words, and they had not been impressed by the French airline's two brief forays into the developing world.

'Doesn't make sense,' said Denis later. 'They told me they spent weeks in the Outback. God, if you knew what hygiene conditions can be like there, you wouldn't touch a thing if you were that picky. Not to mention the flies. But I suppose the food was served by people with white faces, so they knew there was nothing to worry about.'

'I thought you said Franziska had been round Egypt without turning a hair.'

'Well, yeah. I don't understand it. Annette's a lot younger, and I think Franziska must have picked it up from her. I reckon they've been travelling for too long. Culture overload. If I were them I'd just cut it short and go home.'

After another couple of days, during which Annette spent most of her time huddled under a mosquito net reading paperbacks, like a patient in an isolation ward, they went on northwards. Six weeks later Denis received a postcard from Switzerland: *After we leave you we enjoy very much in Kota Bahru, and Penang was so interesting and so nice food. Denis, when we were with you you were not so happy, I think perhaps something in your life is not good. I am so sorry. I hope you are more happy now. Love, Franziska and Annette.*

Denis was speechless for some time. 'Not so happy,' he repeated at last in a strained voice, 'because I was racking my flaming brains trying to think of something that would bring those two wet blankets to life . . . talk about selective amnesia. They must have got over their culture shock here and cheered up as soon as they reached the Kelantan border.'

I had recently designed a cover for the company's Travel Newsletter and been paid with a bottle of more-than-adequate Australian claret, which was sitting on my kitchen shelf waiting for any hint of a celebration. There were also the remains of the previous day's casserole in the fridge.

'Look,' I said, 'why don't you come across and help me demolish all this? You won't mind a few *a-ni-mals* in the rice, will you?'

'Thanks. That's very good of you. Tell you what, I've got a couple of durians. I didn't dare get them out with Franziska and Annette around in case they took one sniff and dropped down dead on the spot. I'll bring them over.'

'Don't the Chinese say you shouldn't mix alcohol and durian?'

'Bollocks,' said Denis. 'That may be true if you drink tumblersful of Rémy Martin all through the meal the way the Chinese do. But wine goes with everything.'

We feasted sitting out on my own small veranda, drinking wine and slurping the foetid-caramel richness of the durian flesh off the massive seeds. I made coffee and lit a cigar as we talked about everything under the sun, or at least under the veiled moon. Around us the invisible cicadas rasped and stridulated in the darkness, and in lulls between our meandering comments we could hear the hushing of the surf.

The Chinese were wrong. Claret and durian went together perfectly well. East and West – at least at certain privileged moments under a soft tropical moon – could coexist after all.

Speaking in Tongues at Telok Lipat

But the coexistence could be heavy going, there was no denying that. The glamour of living in a very different part of the world, the lure of the exotic, only lasts for a certain length of time. A clump of coconut palms, once the novelty has worn off, is not intrinsically more fascinating than a clump of London planes in Kensington Gardens. Sometimes you find yourself looking with a jaded eye at the publicity materials put out by the tourist organisations, trying to square that note of breathlessly willed enchantment with the workaday demands of your own life as you juggle with a job, with domestic routine, with bureaucracy, with the frustrations of dealing with people whose expectations differ, in nameless scarcely-definable ways, from your own.

The tourist comes for a week and sees the film-set, but you stay on in the scrubland acres behind it. The lure of the exotic is like love: it transports you to interesting places, but you have to keep on going under your own steam afterwards.

There were trivial annoyances, like the electric pump which brought my water up from the well behind the house and which frequently used to fail just when it was most needed, leaving me to clean my teeth with only a mugful of water beside an unflushed loo. There were plagues of droppings: gecko-droppings, dark with a white tip like doll's-house cigars, all over the top of the mosquito-net, and anywhere else within reach of the ceiling for that matter; mouse-droppings all over the kitchen, including the grill-pan; periodic cowpats on the sandy ground outside and sometimes underneath the house itself. These encouraged flies, which unlike mosquitoes were not otherwise a nuisance.

I felt quite kindly disposed towards the small brown cattle, but it was a curious sensation to be woken in the middle of the night by the house swaying and almost tilting as though a silent earthquake were in progress. The first time it happened I came near panic; I had once been woken by an earth tremor in Greece and never forgotten the experience. A moment later I realised that it was simply a cow which had wandered between the concrete pillars which held the house up and was scratching its back at leisure on the underside of the wooden floor.

There were other disturbances in the night. Once I blinked my eyes open after only a few minutes of sleep to see an animated spark moving slowly around the room, winking in the darkness. I remember a moment of disorientation, thinking in a blurred sleepy sort of way that something had caught fire from the burning mosquito-coil and that I was watching sparks raining downwards. It resolved itself into a firefly, what a visiting Australian friend of Denis's described as 'a mozzie with landing lights'. I lay and watched it for some time, fascinated.

And then, overshadowing all these, was the single dominating annoyance of religion. I do not know whether what I have written so far gives any real impression of the all-pervading presence of Islam on that coast. Minatory public hoardings and wall-posters reminded you constantly of what you might have mercifully forgotten. Some of them bore quotations from the Koran which were in the equivalent of a Biblical Malay I did not understand, except that they tended to begin *Sesungguhnya* which means something like *Verily, verily*. The one I liked least said SEMBAHYANGLAH SEBELUM ANDA DISEMBAHYANGKAN which means 'Start praying yourself before others are praying for you' – i.e. before you die, or at least before something terrible happens to you. The Faithful were never allowed to forget their faith for long. Nor was anyone else.

There is nominal 'freedom of religion' in Malaysia, which means that Christians, Buddhists and Hindus are officially allowed to follow their various beliefs. As is sometimes pointed out when no-one in authority is listening, the 'freedom of religion' does not extend to the Malays themselves. Muslim converts are welcomed, but a Muslim (and all Malays are defined automatically as Muslim) is not permitted to leave his religion, even to declare himself an agnostic, on pain of all-encompassing social disgrace.

He is also subject to the *Shariah* laws, which mean that in some states he can be whipped for being caught drinking alcohol, and at the least heavily fined if he is caught with a woman in anything which a fevered imagination could imagine to be a compromising situation.

Early in my second year the Teachers' Club went on an outing in the form of a day trip to Kuantan Science School. Fiona had been transferred across the country by now, and I had no personal interest in playing badminton with the staff there, which seemed to be the main purpose of the visit, but I asked if there would be any chance to go shopping. There were things to be had in Kuantan which even enterprising Mr Loo did not run to: wholemeal bread, French cheese, coffee beans.

'Shopping? Of course. The minibus driver can take you in the afternoon.'

Navam, Choo Lay, Lee Kit and a new Chinese teacher called Mei Lin had the same idea, and we piled into the school minibus with enthusiasm. Once we reached Kuantan Science School, which was awkwardly located eight miles out of the town centre, things changed somewhat as the male Muslim majority among the Kuala Penyu teachers asserted its authority. First they had the women's badminton doubles called off (unilaterally) so that the men could fit in a couple of extra games. Then, after we had all hung around for an extra hour in the middle of the day, they commandeered the minibus and its driver to take them across to the school hostel (which was all of two hundred yards away) for their midday prayers.

'But we were supposed to go shopping . . .'

'Shopping . . . ?' The Malay teachers giggled; it was a gesture of either limp embarrassment or deliberate obfuscation which I found more annoying than any other response. 'But we have to pray, you see. And there isn't time anyway . . .'

I choked back the urge to point out that it was they who had used it up. But once they had wrapped their ceremonial sarongs round their middles and piled into the minibus to go and wash their feet at the mosque I was moved to say various bad-tempered things about the Princes of the Soil and the One True Faith to Navam and the Chinese girls. It was a trivial enough incident, but for me it seemed to bring an enormous amount of latent irritation to the surface.

It was particularly irritating to realise that not only could the wishes of a foreigner be discounted because he was a foreigner (which after all has to be accepted as an occupational hazard of working outside your own country), but the wishes of four women could also safely be discounted because they were not only infidels but women.

The girls looked at me with some surprise as I found hitherto unsuspected reserves of invective. 'We have to put up with it,' said Navam with a trace of apology when I had finished my tirade. 'It's really their country, you see.' I saw, but was not mollified.

For me, in my own personal history of acclimatisation and adjustment, it was a significant moment. I had been in Malaysia for a year and a quarter. Logically I suppose I should have got over that surge of uncontrollable annoyance during my first two or three months in the country. You imagine an initial honeymoon period, then a longer period of being routinely settled, with either intermittent stirrings of affection for the place (if you are lucky) or homesickness (if you are less so). The reality is more complicated. I was often very fond of the place, and of the kampong people; it was just that I was paying the price for those fifteen months of self-effacement, of consciously deferring to local expectations, of falling into the role of the even-tempered outsider willing to put up with any amount of discomfort in the interests of retaining local goodwill.

'It's really their country, you see . . .' It had been my attitude exactly. Now, quite suddenly, because of what must have appeared a trivial frustration to anyone else – what did a brief shopping trip matter one way or the other, after all? – I could taste the bile rising in my throat.

Shops stay open late in South-East Asia, so that in the event there would still have been ample time for a quick descent on the Teruntum shopping complex in the centre of the town. But by the time we left the school, between six and seven, I assumed it was too late to mention it again. Presumably everyone would want to get home as quickly as possible. I resigned myself to what I expected would at least be a direct journey: two hours' fast drive up the coast.

It was not to be. Half-way back, with twilight swallowed up in darkness, the minibus stopped at a huge new gold-domed roadside mosque. For the second time that afternoon the Muslim majority poured out to change into its ritual costume, wash its collective feet and perform the complicated obeisances of Islamic prayer. It took them thirty-five minutes. I remembered various uncomplimentary things I had said in the course of my adult life about the Anglican and Roman Catholic churches and regretted them all.

Glowing with virtue, the Muslims emerged from the mosque and took their places again. An hour more on the road. I thought of the simple meal waiting for me at home. It would be good to be back. Half an hour into this final leg of the journey the minibus stopped again. I stared out of the window in sick disbelief.

We had pulled up by a wayside restaurant, and the Muslims, with the nearest approach to jovial laughter they ever managed, were pouring out again. There was a whole half-hour of travelling to go before they reached home, and it must have been all of two and a half hours since the tables had last been spread at Kuantan Science School. They were being asked to probe the limits of human endurance. It had been hungry work, all that praying.

Huge plates of rice heaped with curry and vegetables made their appearance. It was another half hour before we set off again on that final leg of the journey. By the time we reached Kuala Penyu it was ten o'clock at night. Watching the Muslims descend from the minibus I found myself assailed by odd atavistic images of wax figurines and pins. Perhaps I could get hold of some plasticine and try. I was not in an ecumenical mood.

There were frequent religious meetings near my Sura Jetty house. The opposition Islamic Party was trying hard at the time to unseat the government of Dr Mahathir and establish its own joyless equivalent of Ayatollah Khomeini's Iranian theocracy. Its leader, a demagogue called Haji Hadi Awang, had his base at Kampong Rusila, only a few miles up the coast. At the biggest of the meetings the crowd wore green sarongs, the colour sacred to the Prophet. Their white skull-caps bobbed in the lamplit darkness as one or other

speaker delivered an interminable harangue through a battery of temporary loudspeakers. There were enthusiastic, drunken-sounding shouts from the crowd. It might all have been innocent revivalist stuff, but to me the blaring amplified voice and rhythmic responses, punctuated by whining feedback, sounded ominous and obscurely frightening.

When the rally was over and the night was filled with the prolonged anticipatory revving of thoughtlessly-parked cars I put on a cassette of Byrd's Mass in Five Parts. The wall-clock said nearly midnight. *Gloria in excelsis Deo*, sang the voices, while the geckoes chattered on the ceiling and the sound of car engines faded into the night. If Islam had produced anything like that, I found myself thinking, perhaps I would have had more time for it. But it was hard for me at any rate to summon up much warmth of feeling for a religion which appeared to save its strongest condemnation for music, visual art, alcohol and the free meeting of the sexes. If I had been a Muslim that would have left me only books, gardening and travel.

My mind went back to an article I had read in the New Straits Times recently. According to one Dr Sayyid Waqar Ahmed Husaini of the University of Malaya, who appeared to be nothing if not comprehensive in his specifications,

The implications of Islamic medical law for public policy could include a ban on the growing of tobacco and the opium poppy, prohibition on manufacture of carcinogenous food additives, and the discouragement of free mixing of men and women while promoting marriage and wholesome socialisation.

Agnus Dei, sang the voices, *qui tollis peccata mundi*: Lamb of God, who bearest the sins of the world . . . It was a sublime, spacious, utterly ethereal piece of music. And yet Roman Catholicism, when you considered it divested of its artistic excrescences, could be as repressive as Islam. Its history was certainly far more bloodstained. Perhaps some day, I thought, I would see the architecture of Isfahan and be bowled over.

I switched off the cassette player with an agnostic blessing on William Byrd, the choir of Christ Church Cathedral, Oxford, and the harmony of voices, and went to bed.

The Javanese, those teeming anciently-civilised cousins of the Malays to the south-east, called it the Malaysian Disease: this creeping intolerant religious obsession which was at its strongest, most ignorant and least reasonable in the rural north of the peninsula, in Trengganu, Kelantan and Kedah. Travelling through Bandung and Yogyakarta that year I had been amazed by the Indonesian talent for religious coexistence. After the stark dividing-lines of life among the Faithful on the East Coast it was almost shocking to see a shop calling itself 'Christian Book Centre'. Even more to see the large *toko buku* which sell school books and stationery and display works on Islam on their shelves next to Catholic devotional figurines of Our Lady, books about the *Kristen Protestan* religion and crucifixes to hang on the wall.

The Javanese have always had a gift for assimilating beliefs and philosophies, so that remnants of Sanskrit mysticism and native animism jostle the outward forms of Islam. They are proud of the ancient pre-Muslim roots of their civilisation. It is rather like the way European 'Christian' culture is indissolubly mixed up with remnants of pagan festivals and strands from Greek mythology or philosophy. In contrast to the Javanese, the Malays regard their own history as having only begun with the Arab traders who introduced Islam around the fourteenth century.

Outside Javanese bookshops (as in Jalan Malioboro, Yogyakarta) the street vendors sell a range of posters. You can choose between General Suharto, Brooke Shields (who appears to have made a deep impression on the East), an Indonesian pop singer called Rato Karno, a Muslim girl praying against a wall-hanging of the sacred Qa'aba at Mecca, Madonna (the pop singer) and the Madonna herself (with definite article) accompanied by the rest of the Holy Family. No-one would mind if you chose the whole pantheon; that would be the Javanese way.

Two other posters caught my eye in Jalan Malioboro. Both bore prominent lettering. One read, under a saccharine portrait of the head of Christ: YESUS MATI UNTOK KITA, Jesus died for us. The one next to it bore the supreme Muslim invocation ALLAH ALRAHMAN ALRAHIM: God the Compassionate, the Merciful. Such a juxtaposition would be inconceivable in Malaysia where even the Indonesian-Malay translation of the Bible is banned because it uses the word *Allah* for God and is therefore considered blasphemous towards the One True Faith.

Even in relaxed Indonesia the 'Malaysian disease' is making its first symptoms felt in the form of fundamentalist stirrings. In Malaysia it is reaching epidemic proportions, spreading like cloud-shadows across the landscape – far faster than the new oil-palm plantations – from the rural northern states towards the more cosmopolitan West Coast of Kuala Lumpur, Malacca, Ipoh and Penang. Male student doctors refuse to attend women patients. Malay girls across the country are bullied into wearing the *tudong*, the wimple-like head-covering. At the International Islamic University even foreign women lecturers are compelled to cover their heads. Not content with following their own *halal* dietary laws, Malays start to whisper that food which has even been handled at any stage by non-Muslims is unclean and must be shunned by the Faithful. Even a cake which has been cut by a non-believer may be seen as corrupted.

An Indian friend of mine teaching on the East Coast used to have a regular lift into school with a Malay colleague. One day the Malay teacher stopped his car outside the Indian's house without unlocking the passenger door and leaned out of the window. 'Sorry,' he said, 'but people have been talking, and I realise now that it's wrong for me to have an unbeliever in my car. My Muslim friends say it makes it unclean for them. You do understand, don't you?'

He was not even apologetic, except in the most perfunctory way. It was like an up-to-date urban Westerner announcing that he had seen the light at last and decided to ban smoking in his car, or switch to mono-unsaturated cooking oil in the interests of his health-conscious dinner guests. Sorry, cigarette-smokers. Sorry, butter-lovers. Sorry, non-Muslims. It's in the interests of our health, you see.

Indians are the most naturally outspoken people in Malaysia, not being exactly Asians in the sense understood by Malays or Chinese, and it was a Sikh Indian girl I knew who told me another story. It was something she had found both shocking and depressing. She was a teacher at a residential school, not even in the wilds of Trengganu but only an hour's drive from Kuala Lumpur. Strolling past one of the *asramas*, the school dormitory blocks, she had glanced in through the window and seen a group of girls. One of them had just washed her hair, so that her normally balaclava'd and wimpled head was bare while she dried it. But as my friend walked on there came a scream of horror. She turned back and looked in more closely.

The Malay girl, still screaming as though confronted by a giant spider, was frantically trying to cover her head with a towel. She had been seen bare-headed by a non-Muslim, and she was hysterical. Never mind that the point of the

Muslim prohibition on women showing their hair is to avoid appearing needlessly attractive to the opposite sex, which has a certain logic even if you do not accept the premise. Never mind that my friend was a woman, and one of the girl's own teachers at that, *in loco parentis* at a boarding-school. Logic – even inconsistent human logic – was somewhere a long way away. What you had instead, increasingly, was a febrile hysteria. The Faithful had made their religion into a protective pentagram. Islam was clean and safe; outside the magic circle, in a world of defilement, the monsters roamed.

'Malays feel weak,' Adibah Amin had said, 'and religion makes them feel strong.' It had become something like a drug: intoxicating, hallucinatory, capable of breaking down the personality.

One evening Denis and I shared a pavement-table meal in the centre of Kuala Penyu with Selvam, a thoughtful and outspoken Indian from the local hospital staff. 'Fifteen years ago,' he said, 'this was a marvellous country. You could mix together, any race.'

It was something I had heard many times from Chinese, from Indians, from British who had known Malaysia around the time of independence in the mid-sixties. Even allowing for the human tendency to sentimentalise the past in response to unfamiliar new forms of stress, you sensed an element of truth.

Selvam's view, which again is shared by many, was that the May 1969 race riots had directly or indirectly created the racial and hence religious polarisation. Modern Malaysia's short history seemed to be divided into two periods: before and after 1969.

'But it is a beautiful country. It is not the people – they are very *friendly* people – it is the Government policies.'

Selvam went on to develop an original line, which I found interesting. 'Here on the East Coast,' he said, 'the non-Muslims are making things worse for themselves. Because they will not stand up for themselves. They will not do anything which might offend the Muslims. They are always *deferring* to them. And it is not good because the Muslims come to think they are always right, that they can just snap their fingers and everyone will obey. Even if it is something stupid.'

I thought of my outburst at the Science School in Kuantan. And yet what else could an expatriate do but defer? We were only there for a couple of years, or at the most for us as long as our company's contract with the Ministry was renewed, and the Government would have had no hesitation in kicking anyone it saw as a troublemaker out of the country. Deference was the order of the day, or of the two years.

It was the Malaysian Indians and the Chinese I felt sorry for. They had no foreign bolt-holes waiting for them, except those enterprising renegades who had managed to ease their way into Canada or America or Australia in the anticipation of a gloomy future at home.

Mei Lin, the new Chinese teacher I mentioned, was a devout Christian, and she and her friend Sharon (they were a cheerful, friendly pair) sometimes used to hint that I might like to pay a visit to the new Elim church. I had always smiled rather evasively at this, having an agnostic's distrust of revivalist Christianity. At the same time I had felt occasional stirrings of curiosity. What sort of thing had gone on at 4F Jalan Nibong, beneath the Chart of the Course of Time from Eternity to Eternity, before Jim and I had come to lower the tone? And perhaps also it was an overdose of prickly intolerant Islam which occasionally stirred a feeling of nostalgia for my own ancestral culture. I felt I owed it to my upbringing to go to church at least occasionally. When Mei Lin invited me to the new premises in Telok Lipat for a meal and service, I accepted.

The service conformed to local custom by being held on a Friday. It and the evening meal which preceded it were in commemoration of Sister Paukku who was retiring to Finland after setting up the church in Kuala Penyu and staying with it for twenty-five years.

The new church turned out to be the ground floor of a

modern white cement shop-house, one of a row in a side-road not far from Mr Wong's driving school. Inside, it was like an English church hall. There were rows of metal seats, with a dais at the far end backed by curtains, like a stage. There was a Sunday School notice-board and a banner overhead which said in brightly coloured Irish uncial lettering THIS IS OUR 25TH ANNIVERSARY. One of the few Chinese sixth formers from school was there, along with two unfamiliar Europeans, a sprinkling of Tamils and a visiting Indonesian minister. Otherwise, except for myself and of course the two Finnish ladies it was very much a Chinese congregation.

We began with a buffet spread of food: *gulai ayam* which is a kind of chicken stew, *nasi minyak* which is rice cooked with oil, and the big puffy prawn crackers called *keropok*, with a slice of watermelon to follow.

'How long do you think it'll last?' I asked Mei Lin as we slurped watermelon. It had been a busy week, and I was tired. I was not clear what I had committed myself to.

'Oh, I should think an hour and a half, something like that.'

An hour and a half of hymns and sermons seemed a reasonable return for a plate of *gulai ayam*. Lee Kit, who was also there, was less hopeful. 'Maybe nearer three hours,' she said.

My heart began to sink. But there was no chance to make any further enquiries, because the rows of metal chairs were already filling up. I took my place towards the back, next to an elderly Chinese who gave me a smile of intense enthusiasm which I found faintly disconcerting. It turned out later that though he now lived in Singapore he was one of the founder-members of the Kuala Penyu church, and made the 300-mile journey every couple of months.

The service started reasonably enough, with two jolly revivalist hymns (or 'songs', as they were called here) with the kind of tonic-dominant tunes you can pick up by the third stanza or so. We sang:

> *O perfect redemption, the purchase of blood!*
> *To every believer the promise of God;*
> *The vilest offender who truly believes*
> *That moment from Jesus a pardon receives.*

It was good rousing stuff, with a loudly strummed guitar and jingling tambourine to jolly up the treacly pulsing of the electronic organ. The elderly Chinese next to me, who spoke no English, joined in tunelessly and (inevitably) more or less wordlessly, but with gusto:

> *And then one day I'll cross Death's river,*
> *I'll fight Life's final war with Pain,*
> *But then as Death gives way to Victory*
> *I'll see the light of glory*
> *And I'll know He reigns.*

We sat down, glowing with exertion despite the air-conditioning. Groups of children processed to the dais and sang two more songs, one in English, another in Malay. The pastor was a Chinese from Kuala Lumpur with a thin face and long lank hair which gave him the aesthetic under-nourished look of an eighteen-nineties poet.

His sermon was translated sentence by sentence into Mandarin, like everything else in the service except the songs, by a Chinese interpreter standing beside him. The interpreter gulped orange squash in the occasional interlude of song; there was a throat-constricting amount to translate into the lilting sibilance of Mandarin, and he seemed to be suffering. I learned in passing that the word for 'faith' is *singsing*; it began almost every sentence in the Minister's address.

More children sang, and the interpreter mopped his brow. 'Now,' said the aesthetic-looking pastor, 'I invite you all to pray to the Lord in your own way.'

This sounded puzzling. At first, as we knelt, there was the usual hushed silence. Then after a couple of minutes little eerie whispers and hissings and moans started to spread through the church, like the ghosts in *Julius Caesar* squeaking and gibbering. The congregation were speaking, or at least muttering under their breath, in tongues.

Suddenly the man from Singapore beside me threw his head back and began to shout at the top of his voice. It sounded to me like an outbreak of delirium, a chaotic yelling which refused to resolve itself into anything my ears could accept as a human utterance. I took it for a Pentecostal tongue, but afterwards Mei Lin told me he had merely been giving thanks to God in Hokkien Chinese.

He babbled on in this way for seven or eight minutes, barely pausing to gasp for breath, yelling and half-sobbing in torrents of sound. Behind this solo outpouring, like something created by the BBC Electronic Special Effects Department, the eerie muttering and moaning ebbed and flowed in the background.

Without warning the special effects subsided and we sank back on to our seats. There was a reference to 'various speakers to come'. The first of these was another Chinese pastor, older and jollier-looking, more like a Wakey-Wakey holiday camp attendant than a decadent poet. His sermon was punchy stuff, largely about the fact that we were all Children of Abraham and therefore Children of Faith ('*Singsing,*' gabbled the interpreter). When he was convinced that we had grasped the point he shifted gear and told the story of how the Apostle Paul had gone to heaven for five days.

The audience seemed to be enjoying it, and the numerous children present laughed at all the right moments, as far as I could tell. They were well-behaved and good-humoured, which I was prepared to accept as evidence that the whole business must have had its heart in the right place. But I was bewildered by the sermon; it was as though I had missed some all-important sentence which would have explained the connection between it all. Why did St Paul's miraculous ascension prove that we were Children of Abraham? And what did that have to do with Faith?

Obviously I was expecting the wrong kind of logic. Or perhaps it was all clearer in Mandarin. As far as the rest of the congregation was concerned it all seemed to be working on a subliminal level, like the kind of political speech which gets the audience on its feet by strategic references to *Ten years of Tory misrule* or *The vested interests of the parasitic bourgeoisie*.

After this a group of young adults, including Mei Lin, processed to the front and sang another song to the guitar, in Mandarin this time. I could see the Indonesian pastor stirring in the wings and remembered the reference to *speakers to come*, in the plural. Perhaps all the Pentecostal pastors of tropical Asia were gathered there waiting their turn.

I glanced surreptitiously at my watch. By now it was approaching nine o'clock. I had been at the service for three hours and my limited Friday-night stamina was at a low ebb. I slipped out quietly and rode the three miles home along the beach road, turning off it to follow the sandy track between the coconut palms whose trunks loomed pale in the motorbike headlight. Small monitor lizards scattered across the sand as I passed.

I made tea and slumped into a chair. My radio-cassette-player was being repaired, so there was no music or World Service to obscure the sounds of Kampong Sura and the house itself. The wall-clock ticked and the usual invisible population of cicadas shrilled faintly. On the darkened common a distressed cow lurked, calling out *Mbuuuh* every ten seconds. It might have lost its calf. Or perhaps it was a Pentecostal cow.

As I drank my tea the shrilling of the cicadas grew louder, like the sound of wind whistling in telegraph wires. Through the frosted-glass slats of the window I could see flames flickering as a bonfire of household rubbish burned within the blackness. From a veranda over the way came the faint sound of Malay voices.

The blaring cow receded into the distance. It was not a Pentecostal cow at all. It was a Western cow, as seen from an Asian point of view: an essentially herd animal with strong family instincts which had lost either its way, its herd, its parent or its child, or all of these things. Herdless, without family, a long way from familiar points of reference, I felt a certain kinship with it.

MALAY HISTORY MADE SIMPLE

They scratched the edges of the land
But let the ancient forests stand.
Then men with hungry faces came;
Their land was never quite the same.

The British rulers came and went,
Their conquering energy all spent.
The Chinese traders came to stay,
Growing richer every day.

No sooner were the treaties signed
Than buildings rose and tin was mined
(The earth gouged out to yield its ore),
And still the strangers wanted more.

By the once-placid riverside
In fear they watched the rising tide
As changes spread across the land
Too fast for them to understand.

Excluded from the process, some
Dream secretly, with prayer and drum,
That everything God did not say
Is false, will be destroyed some day.

East Coast to East Coast

The rain was pouring down. The Chinese lorry-driver and I took shelter on my veranda while I signed the invoice for the removal company. 'Where rest of your family?' he asked.
  'No family. Only me.'

'Only you? Family in your own country?'
'No. Not married.'

His smile broadened. 'Aaa . . . *bachelor?*' The two Malay assistants laughed.

Apart form the suite of rattan furniture there were a desk, a tin trunk and twelve cardboard boxes to be taken away. I watched the Malay assistants stretching a tarpaulin over what I could not help seeing as the bleeding dismembered remnants of my household. The company from Kuantan had sent a huge open lorry big enough to take my entire house, if there had been a crane handy to lift it off its concrete pillars.

Looking round the bare, rather dusty woodwork of 59A Jalan Kenanga when the removal men had driven away in the rain I found it hard to imagine that it had ever been a comfortable home. It was simply a box, not unlike the twelve other boxes I had watched being loaded on to the lorry, only several sizes larger. It was like seeing a clever deception revealed. Moving is a melancholy business, especially when you are on your own.

That evening Hasnah, the girl who ran the little Malay store down the lane, called at my house with her mother to look at the fridge and gas cooker I was trying to sell. We bargained for a while, with much smiling on both sides. I opened the fridge door so that they could take a look inside.

'Of course,' said the old woman, smiling so persistently I knew she was worried, 'it hasn't had anything *haram* in it, has it – anything forbidden to Muslims?'

The spectre of a giant malevolent pig suddenly loomed over the kitchen, threatening the hopeful deal. '*Bukan, bukan,*' I said, quick as a flash. 'Course not.'

Which was a diplomatic lie, as there was the best part of half a pound of bacon sitting on the meat shelf where I had had the sense to hide it in a white plastic bag, reserved for my last meal before the cooker was sold. I was beginning to lose patience with Muslim sensitivities.

The price we eventually settled on left something to be desired, but for a last-minute sale (my previous arrangement had fallen through a couple of days before) it was not too humiliating. The following day, with the bacon safely inside me and the interior of the fridge sluiced out with bleach and detergent, Hasnah came back with a bicycle-rickshaw driver. Fridge and cooker-top (two burners and a grill-pan; nobody in Malaysia has any use for an oven) were loaded on to the bathchair arrangement of the trishaw with its hood pushed back like that of a baby's pram in fine weather.

The driver started to wheel the contraption towards Hasnah's shop several hundred yards away.

'*Becak yang kuat!*' I said. 'Pretty strong rickshaw!' Hasnah and the driver both laughed. I felt ridiculously pleased. Nothing is better for the ego than making even the feeblest joke in a foreign language. It had taken me two years of intermittent struggling to reach that point.

By the following morning, my last in Kuala Penyu, there was nothing much left in the house except the single dangerous-looking portable electric ring I had inherited from Jim a year before and never had occasion to use till then. I brewed tea on this and breakfasted without enthusiasm on a lump of already sweating Gouda cheese and a leftover mandarin orange. My landlady Wan, broom in hand and children in tow, wandered through the house with a proprietorial air Six-year-old Sukirman strutted past shrieking with precocious laughter, clutching one end of a massive stick like a shillelagh against his groin so that it thrust obscenely upwards and outwards with its other end almost at the level of his shoulders. Acha, the tiny mite of a girl who was his frequent companion, watched him with shy admiration. I had the impression that at the kampong level Malay life was not always the priggishly virtuous business emphasised by teachers, politicians and newspaper commentators.

I had sorted out everything as best I could, with the result that tying up the loose ends of a two-year stay in the country had left me feeling drained and mildly apprehensive. It was the sort of mood in which you imagine yourself missing your connections, or being detained at the airport because something is wrong with your visa.

Among other things I had had to retrieve various of my

possessions. Several weeks before, Sukirman had asked if he could take my ancient binoculars next door to show his sister Zam. I had waited in vain for their return. In the end, with most of my belongings packed, I had been forced to walk across to Wan's house and ask for them back.

Wan was gently evasive. 'Sukirman said you told him he could keep them.'

It was an awkward moment. I knew the family were seeing how far they could stretch my goodwill, which was mildly annoying considering I was already leaving them all sorts of things, but I did not wish to give offence. I had enjoyed living in the house, and I felt perfectly well-disposed towards them all. I constructed a sentence with great care.

'They . . . belonged to my father. Now my father is dead, so they are very . . . very important to me. *Macam cenderamata*, like a souvenir.'

It was true, which was probably why I managed to find the words in Malay without too much difficulty. Telling a lie in a foreign language is even harder than making a joke, which did not stop me having managed both in twenty-four hours. Zam fetched me the binoculars, smiling ambiguously. The smile might have represented goodwill, it might have been merely embarrassment.

The final lingering difficulty had been the curious business of the telephone. I had not been able to transfer it from Jalan Nibong to the Sura Jetty house because there were no lines available at that end of the town yet, so before I left Rasul's enclave I had walked round to the Telekom headquarters and asked to have it disconnected and the account terminated. I remembered a cheerful Telekom employee coming across and bodily removing the whole installation. I knew there was a final thirty dollars or so to pay, but the bill was not ready yet. I suggested that they should take it out of my hundred dollars deposit and refund me the balance at their leisure.

For the first eight months of the year I had heard nothing. After this, to my dismay, the first of a series of new bills was passed on to me at Sura Jetty by the people who had moved into 4F Jalan Nibong. The phantom telephone had gone on chalking up charges, in the way that an amputated limb is said to give its ex-owner phantom twinges now and then. Ninety . . . a hundred and thirty . . . finally, in October, nearly two hundred dollars, and no mention of any deposit to be refunded.

It was disconcerting. Was it an oversight on the part of Telekom, or had smooth *Tuan* Rasul had the instrument reconnected for his new tenants under my own name?

I sought advice from Malaysian colleagues at school. The consensus was that this was a time for Asian evasiveness rather than European bluster. In the end I slipped away without making further enquiries. It was a pity about the seventy dollars or so I had assumed I had owing to me, but in my mildly paranoiac end-of-contract exhaustion I was terrified of being trapped in bureaucratic flypaper at the last moment, with my air ticket confirmed and paid for.

To be on the road again, in a taxi speeding down the coast to Kuantan and from there to the airport at Kuala Lumpur, was intoxicating. The rampant vegetation of the wayside had never seemed greener or more richly varied. Everything in the landscape, even the dreary little town of Chukai, took on an extraordinary originality now that there was nothing routine about it any longer.

It would have been nice to have been able to write about how tears of pure affection welled up in my eyes as I looked at these things for the last time, but I did not really feel like that at all. I knew perfectly well that nostalgia would come later, but for the moment the only thing I was vividly aware of was my own sense of freedom. Everything along the road to Kuantan joined in a gigantic song, and I hummed along with it. I felt as though I was drunk, but it was only the combination of exhaustion and relief that the whole complicated, demanding business of leaving had sorted itself out against all the odds.

No more Trengganu Islam. No more smug ignorant politicians uttering self-righteous platitudes or inept threats. I had kept a folder of newspaper headlines which set the tone:

STOP THIS PRACTICE: DR M. JUNIOR PWD STAFF RAPPED. SANUSI RAPS MEMBERS WHO CAUSE DISUNITY. DR M. RAPS CRITICS OF ANTI-POVERTY MEASURES. STUDENTS RAPPED FOR CHANGING THEIR CITIZENSHIP. MTUC RAPS AUSSIES FOR RAISING FEES. TOE THE LINE OR GET OUT, SETTLERS TOLD. MUSA TELLS UN: GET MOVING.

East Asians are fond of pointing out proudly how in their kind of politics, consensus is vastly more important than Western-style confrontation. What they fail to add is that this democratic-sounding 'consensus' is dominated and steamrollered by leaders of extraordinary arrogance. Even a conspicuously humane and civilised figure like Musa Hitam (mentioned above as telling the UN to get a move on) is made to appear arrogant by the toadying style of reporting which Malaysian (and Singaporean) politicians encourage. Mrs Thatcher, as reported via the Guardian Weekly or the BBC World Service, came across as gentle and tactful in comparison.

The most extraordinary case had been that of the Minister for Information, Rais Yatim. One of the New York orchestras – I think the Philharmonic – had planned to give a concert in Kuala Lumpur as part of an Asia-Pacific tour. The prospect had caused great excitement in music-loving circles in Malaysia, where Western popular culture is widely embraced but Western 'high culture' is very much the preserve of a beleaguered minority.

The orchestra had sent on its programme in advance. One of the works on it was a twentieth-century piece for cello and orchestra, *Schelomo* by Ernst Bloch. Bloch, as I dimly remembered, was a Swiss Jew who later emigrated to America, and *Schelomo* (i.e. 'Solomon') is a loving tribute to ancient Hebrew legend. I had heard it on the radio once, years before, in England. I remembered it dimly as a sombre, melancholy, rather powerful work with an Oriental cast to some of its melodies, ironically in the same way as Malay music which has Arab roots and can sound oddly Middle- or Near-Eastern.

The Minister for Information studied the programme and wrote back to New York that music with a Zionist, or even a Jewish, connection, would be unacceptable in a country whose official religion was Islam and which was solidly behind the struggle of the Palestinian people for self-determination. They were to substitute something more acceptable without delay.

Nobody had told Datuk Rais about the dominant ethnic colouring of the New York classical music scene. The Philharmonic Orchestra understandably took the huff, muttered darkly about anti-semitism and went to Singapore instead. Muslim Malaysia had been preserved at the last moment from another Mossad plot, and Datuk Rais gratefully accepted the plaudits of the Faithful. RAIS RAPS ZIONIST BAND, as the New Straits Times might well have phrased it.

In some ways, paradoxically, it was a pity that English still played such an important part in journalism. What would otherwise have been a struggling but useful exercise in Malay reading comprehension and vocabulary-building became a source of annoyance as the crass, sometimes poisonous idiocies of those in power lay nakedly revealed in a language I understood all too well. If I had been unable to understand the newspapers I might never have come to feel so personally about it all.

Towards the end of my time in Malaysia I tried to compose my annoyance in the form of a short article. Three years later I can see that it is not without its own element of aggrieved self-righteousness. Re-reading it I am also struck by how soon any attempt to be specific about popular culture becomes dated. Who on earth was Boy George? people will soon be asking. And does anyone still bother with breakdancing?

I called the article:

> When I hear the phrase 'Western Culture'
> I reach for my gun

Let me begin by saying that I like living in South-East Asia, that in some ways it feels to me a saner and more hopeful place than Europe. I say this just in case anyone chooses to misinterpret what follows as merely the grumblings of one more Westerner who thinks that everything is better where he comes from.

I was once talking to a Malaysian colleague about that whole phenomenon which began, I suppose, with Elvis Presley in the fifties and whose current manifestations include Boy George and breakdancing. 'In fact,' I said, 'the whole business of pop culture.'

'Pop culture?' she said. 'What do you mean by that?'

I explained. Comprehension dawned.

'Oh,' she said, 'you mean *Western* culture.'

I came across a number of references to this phenomenon when I first came to live in Asia. After a while the image began to form in my mind of a many-tentacled monster, hidden somewhere the other side of the Gobi Desert and the Himalayas, spreading its malign influence towards the innocent unspoiled inhabitants of East Asia, a hypodermic syringe full of heroin in one hand and all the enticements of materialism in the other.

Surely it's time by now that people in Asia started to use some more neutral phrase: 'pop culture' if you like, 'international culture', even 'junk culture'. But I do begin to bristle a bit when I hear it being tacitly assumed that my own culture — representative democracy, Shakespeare, Bach, Mozart, French wine, the Italian Renaissance and the great cathedrals of Europe notwithstanding — is chiefly notable for having corrupted the rest of the world with such junk fodder as *Dallas*, *Dynasty* and the appalling *Life-styles of the Rich and Famous*.

Always behind these references I sense the comforting implication that Asians, compared with greedy, self-centred Westerners, are a people innocent of materialism, deeply spiritual, selflessly devoted to their families. Of course, there is some truth in this; a visiting Westerner can be profoundly impressed by the family loyalty and generosity of Asians, by their own enduring cultures and traditions. But smug talk of corrupting 'Western culture' should not be used to disguise the fact that there are uniquely Asian kinds of materialism, or selfishness, which can shock even a Westerner: the large-scale pirating of the song 'Don't they know it's Christmas?' for example – for private profit and not for famine relief.

'Western' materialism?' In East Asia there can be a concern with 'conspicuous consumption' and status symbols which makes the poor old British, for example, seem like a bunch of unworldly simple-lifers.

'Western' culture? 'Western' values? Asians avidly read supposedly literate newspapers which consist almost entirely of articles on *Dallas* and *Dynasty* and the whole dream-world of vulgar affluence that goes with them. They then turn round and blame the West for feeding them a diet of materialism. Well, I dare say the West would be just as happy to sell the East symphonic concerts, books on philosophy and videos of the BBC Shakespeare series, if affluent Asia showed much interest in these.

Affluent Asia, however, prefers to make its own selection from the products on offer. This leaves it free to blame the West for producing nothing but the junk it has carefully selected.

This sounds to me rather as though a Westerner, bearing in mind the popularity of the massage-parlours of Bangkok, were to blame the Thais for corrupting the innocent Western (and, of course, Japanese) tourists who come to purchase their pleasures there. I think most of us would recognise this as special pleading; if anything or anybody needs to be blamed, it is surely the appetites of those visitors who are creating the demand. And as long as there is a demand for gratification somebody, somewhere, will be supplying the means for it.

No: all the evidence points to the unpalatable fact that Asians, Anglo-Saxons, Arabs, Africans and Americans, as soon as they acquire wealth, develop an appetite for much the same kinds of thing. They need no prompting from any single part of the world to do so. We are all in this together, in fact. The society we are creating may be a corrupt one in some ways, but for better or worse it is an international one, and the corruption has an international dimension.

A street robber or a syndicate of drug smugglers may as easily be Asian as European or American; so may a medical mission or a fund for famine relief. There's no room for smugness any longer, either Eastern or Western.

As I stood burdened with luggage on the escalator at Holborn underground a young woman pushed roughly past me on her way down to the platforms. 'Don't you know you're supposed to stand on the right?' she shouted.

Judging by her neutral accent she was not an untutored product of the slums but part of Mrs Thatcher's new graceless middle class. I could see there were things I was going to have to get used to all over again.

All that Asian-style smiling at children, for instance: that would have to stop. I could see myself being marked out as a scheming paedophile rapist. And what had happened to the prevailing Puritanism, Chinese Confucian as well as Malay Muslim, which I had grown used to? On the train out of London, fascinated, I picked out headlines in the tabloid newspapers other travellers were reading. Could this be the same planet? HOODED TORY MP IN SEX TORTURE CHAMBER, said one. Another read I HAVEN'T GOT A BIG BUM, SAYS TV ACTRESS.

I tried to read the copy of the Independent I had bought at the station, the first issue of that excellent paper I had ever seen, but it was no use. After what I was used to it was simply too dense, too varied, too thoughtful to take in. The only news I did manage to grasp was that Robert Graves and Philip Larkin had both died in the same week, which was more than enough to cope with. I looked across at my neighbour's paper, which was open with the Problem Page facing me. THREE-IN-BED SEX WITH LOVER AND WIFE, said the headline above the week's star problem. I gave up and stared out of the window.

A low veiled winter sun hung over the fields of Essex. It hung there, lingering as no tropical sun ever could at that angle in the sky, for most of the journey, a cool gentle magical un-tropical light on the fields of grey-brown earth. Why did people in the temperate world sometimes imagine the tropics had a monopoly of beauty? Britain seemed to me, in my current exhausted-traveller's mood of equanimity, something like the castle-city of Gormenghast in Mervyn Peake's trilogy: an ancient claustrophobic place of great, if miasmal, beauty, which I could not imagine returning to whole-heartedly and yet (like Titus with his own birthplace) knew I would never quite break free from.

The ticket inspector paused beside me as he handed back my Whitesaver Return. His smile was understated, faintly ironic, very English. I was back in a country where there was an edge of mockery, of defensiveness, to people's humour. I enjoyed the flavour. The food in England might be bland (as Asians liked to comment), but there was a certain spiciness to everyday social life.

'Bet yew di'n' git that tan in Yarmouth, did yer?' he said in the lilting jerky accent of Suffolk.

Whatever the condition of England as a whole in the mid-nineteen-eighties, East Anglia seemed to have kept some reserves of good-humoured sanity. The train was approaching Woodbridge with its array of boats, muddy estuary and outcrop of rising woodland on the far shore. A few miles beyond that wooded bluff was a different East Coast. I was back home, I supposed.